UNION STATION

A Decorative History of Washington's Grand Terminal

CAROL M. HIGHSMITH AND TED LANDPHAIR

FEATURING PHOTOGRAPHS BY CAROL M. HIGHSMITH

CHELSEA PUBLISHING, INC., WASHINGTON, D.C.

Union Station: A Decorative History of Washington's Grand Terminal

Smith T. Wood
Jackie Fleisher Wood
Chelsea Publishing, Inc.
3299 K. St., NW.
Washington, D.C. 20005

Cover and text design: Meadows & Wiser, Washington, D.C.
Compositor: Carver PhotoComposition, Inc., Arlington, Va.
Printer and binder: Graphtec, Inc., Woodlawn, Md.

ISBN: 0–9620877–0–X

Acknowledgements: The authors extend special appreciation to Herbert H. Harwood, former chief commercial administrator of the Chesapeake & Ohio system and interim director of the Baltimore & Ohio train museum in Baltimore for sharing his considerable expertise on the railroad that formed half of the Washington Terminal Co. ownership. Similarly, Robert Emerson, director of the Railroad Museum of Pennsylvania in Strasburg, provided invaluable leads and information on the "Pennsylvania Railroad half" of terminal history. Superb rail historian John P. Hankey of the University of Delaware graciously shared memorabilia from his collection of railroad mementos and gave the manuscript a sound railroader's inspection before the final "all aboard." Keith Kelly, president of the Union Station Redevelopment Corporation, opened his files and bountiful expertise to make the project possible. Stan Bagley, Amtrak's general superintendent in Washington, kindly made both board of directors records and many of his capable staff of veteran trainmen available to the authors, leading to many of the most memorable anecdotes in this volume. All whose reminiscences are recited herein were generous with their time and interest, and we are especially grateful to retired Interior Department executive Richard R. Hite, who helped sort out the confusing and controversial days when Union Station became the National Visitor Center. Special thanks, too, to streetcar expert LeRoy O. King, Jr.; to veteran Washington Terminal Company engineer (and excellent amateur photographer) William R. Hutson; and to the capable people at the Martin Luther King Library (especially Washingtoniana Division chief Roxanna Deane), the Library of Congress, Imagefinders, Inc., and the Columbia Historical Society for their assistance in locating historic photographs. A tip of the trainman's cap, too, to Helene and Barry Mankowitz for their research support and to Wayne Glass and Robert Bachman for eagle-eyed copyreading. The authors salute designer Robert Wiser for his consummate skill and indefatiguable effort in showcasing this work, and thank Carol M. Highsmith Photography associates David Patterson, Dorothy M. Jones, Jane M. Dow, and John Anderson for their untiring contributions.

The authors. Carol M. Highsmith is a Washington architectural photographer whose lens has documented several monumental renovation projects. Her exhibition on the reopening of the restored Willard Hotel was placed on national tour by the American Institute of Architects. She and her husband, Ted Landphair, a Washington writer and editor, also co-authored *Pennsylvania Avenue: America's Main Street*, featuring Highsmith photographs of the Avenue of the Presidents.

Endleaves. *Three Union Station switching engines pull cars to the coach yard for cleaning or to the Ivy City carshop for repairs. The pristine condition of the tracks and manicure of the ballast in this photo give away the era: very soon after Union Station opened. (LeRoy O. King, Jr. Collection)*

Frontice. *When it opened in 1907, Union Station's 760-ft. Concourse, which was open to train platforms, was the largest room in the world. The B&O's Royal Limited was one of its premier "Royal Blue" trains. (Prints & Photographs Division, Library of Congress)*

Pages 6–7. *An early, posed photograph of the Union Station waiting room, looking toward the West Hall and showing off the terminal's ponderous mahogany benches, equipped with steam heaters. (Prints & Photographs Division, Library of Congress)*

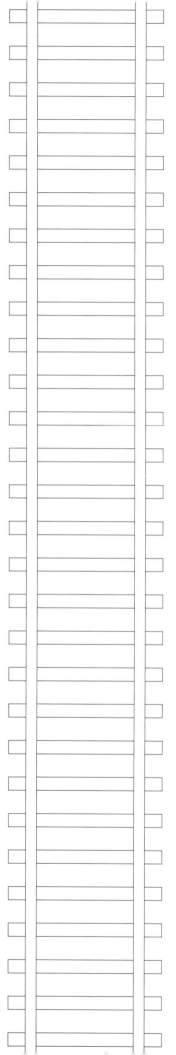

CONTENTS

INTRODUCTION

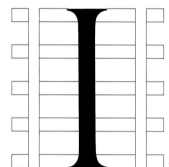

If, on February 28, 1903, as he signed "an Act to provide for a union station in the District of Columbia, and for other purposes," President Theodore Roosevelt could have known to what "other purposes" the station would one day come, he might have at least sighed before signing. If the turn-of-the-century political chiefs who made Union Station the keystone of their beautifying "Washington Plan" had divined that Orville and Wilbur Wright would achieve powered flight 10 months later — and known what that wobbly flight would ultimately mean to train travel — they might have scaled back, if not their blueprints, their rhetoric.

But the railroads were king in 1903, and so they commissioned an imperial transportation palace. From its grandeur to its dowdy decline and second coming, this is Union Station's story. Prominent Washington architectural photographer Carol M. Highsmith spent parts of five years documenting the pathetic dilapidation, and the painstaking rehabilitation, of this titanic building in the 1980s. Other collections produced memorable and historic photographs as well. As the long and tortuous life of Daniel Burnham's transportation palace unfolds in these pages, *Union Station: A Decorative History* may serve as its own preservationist's tool, keeping grand memories alive.

A new central kiosk takes shape in the Main Hall during the 1980s resurrection of Union Station as a train terminal and multilevel shopping arcade. Plans had called for three other such intrusions in the grand, old waiting room, but the city's Council on Historic Preservation, which must countenance renovations in historic landmarks, knocked the number down to one. Most commercial activity would be confined to side halls, various alcove spaces, and, especially, to the old train concourse, which was not as ornate as this room. (Carol M. Highsmith, Photographer)

Above. *Foreman Paul Levidiopis of the restoration contractor, the Barianos Company, pours a plaster mixture into a mold, under the eye of apprentice Mike Halwick. When the plaster forms but has not completely dried, a template is pulled across it, creating the pattern to fit the section of ceiling or wall to be restored. Excess plaster is then chipped off so that the molded piece fits snugly. Other Barianos artisans would later add artistic touches, such as painted traceries or gold leaf, to match the original design from Union Station's halcyon days. (Carol M. Highsmith, Photographer)*

Right. *The station's old train concourse is reshaped into three shopping levels during reclamation by the Union Station Redevelopment Corporation. The beginnings of a gallery level are forming, and work proceeds on the main and basement levels. Portions of the roof are cut out and strengthened, and the huge room takes on a scrubbed appearance never seen in the dingy, dim-lit days of heavy train travel. Under the new configuration, passengers would have the option of lingering or bypassing the retail space for a quick dash to a train. (Carol M. Highsmith, Photographer)*

Master restoration specialist John Barianos (white shirt) and apprentice Apostolos Papadimitris apply delicate leafing to a grand eagle in an alcove of the terminal's Presidential Suite. For years the eagle had hovered in faded red, gold, and blue. Attractive though that color scheme had once been, Barianos followed the dictum of a faithful preservationist—restoring the emblem to the original white-with-silver-leafing Burnham design. (Carol M. Highsmith, Photographer)

Opposite. *Traffic lights change on Columbus Circle at the point where a stub of Delaware Avenue intersects Massachusetts Avenue. Massachusetts was one of three slashing radials across Washington sketched by Pierre L'Enfant. Pennsylvania and New York avenues are the others. The reclamation of Union Station began what many city planners foresaw as a "barbell effect" along "Mass Ave." Growth had already sprouted eastward from trendy Dupont Circle, and it was beginning to work westward from the revitalized node around Union Station as well. (Carol M. Highsmith, Photographer)*

Above. *Christopher Columbus was much on the mind of the nation at the time Union Station was designed. The World's Columbian Exposition in Chicago in 1893 had been a stunning architectural high-water mark. On Lorado Taft's Columbus statue, dedicated in 1912, the New World is depicted by the figure on the left (note her quiver and arrows), the Old World on the right. The explorer who brought the two together stands stiffly between them. (Carol M. Highsmith, Photographer)*

Overleaf: *A traveler arriving by train and passing through the gates of Union Station "immediately gets a proper attitude toward the importance of Washington," wrote* The Washington Sketch Book *in 1935. After an interim in which the soiled, misused, then abandoned terminal cast a melancholy pall over the monumental city, it sprang back to life in the late 1980s as the upgraded southern terminus of Amtrak's Northeast Corridor. The days are long gone when the neighborhood was the decrepit and dangerous Swampoodle. (Carol M. Highsmith, Photographer)*

WHERE THE IDLE GATHERED

In this view, looking west down the front arcade's series of groin vaults to the West Portico, one can appreciate the timeless touch of Daniel Burnham's classic design—and almost picture a medieval time warp: a choir of monks, a gathering of knights, or a wooden oxcart arriving with a load of grain. A few of the ornamental lamp fixtures on the terminal's shadowy east end were lost to souvenir hunters during the days when the station lay fallow, but most others were saved and lovingly restored. (Carol M. Highsmith, Photographer)

In 1800 America's new capital was a horse-and-mule town. Stagecoaches carried 100 passengers a day, at most, from Willard's and Brown's hotels through the woods north of Massachusetts Avenue to the Maryland town of Bladensburg, thence, toilsomely, to Baltimore. Even as the Baltimore & Ohio Railroad was first thrusting westward from Maryland's big port city in 1828, sedentary Washington was pinning its hopes on water transit: packet boats up the Potomac and barges on the fetid city canal and on the new Chesapeake & Ohio Canal to "the West."

But when the Maryland General Assembly authorized a B&O line to Bladensburg, shrewdly higgling a 20-percent cut of passenger revenues for its troubles, Washington could no longer keep the railroad out; Congress approved an extention to a makeshift depot in an old tailor's shop on Pennsylvania Avenue, a locomotive-plume's distance from the Capitol. In 1835, about 800 citizens gathered to greet the B&O trains, pulled by 12-horsepower steam engines aptly christened the "Washington," "Adams," "Jefferson," and "Madison."

The B&O kept Baltimore time, several minutes off Washington's reckoning by the sun, and capital city locals who consulted their timepieces risked missing their trains. Helpfully, a giant bell hallooed each departure. It was one of many annoyances to the depot's neighbor, the United States Congress, which soon introduced a bill declaring the place "a nuisance, where the idle gathered." More because departures had swelled to six a day, freight business was booming, and it had outgrown what an observer called its "filthy" row-house depot, the B&O in 1858 moved a few blocks northeastward, to an elaborate new Italianate building modeled after the railroad's Baltimore terminal. The station on Pennsylvania Avenue quickly became a tavern.

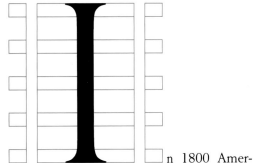

Early passenger coupon books and timetables were sometimes ornate and served to promote the line's service; many have become collectors' treasures. This design enhanced a Pennsylvania Railroad Boston-to-Washington routeguide and timetable. (Warshaw Collection, Smithsonian Museum of American History)

Below. *Looking at the bucolic setting behind the B&O's second terminal at New Jersey Avenue and C Street NW as the New York Seventy-First Regiment arrives in 1861, it's hard to believe that the depot sat two blocks from the U.S. Capitol, which was busy getting domed at the time. Doubtless the artist took liberties with the skyline. Washington was the key point of connection for troops moving south into battle, and Civil War Washington was a sea of blue (and a cloud of dust from all the marching). (Library of Congress)*

Right. *Washington's first depot on Pennsylvania Avenue was hardly imposing. The Baltimore & Ohio Railroad parked its steam engines and open cars behind this converted tailor's shop and, sometime after this sketch was rendered, erected a belfry with which to peal arrivals and departures. Early trains crossed city streets at grade, spooking dray horses and menacing human life and limb. For a time, capital commissioners required that the iron horses stop at the city line and be drawn slowly by horses into the Pennsylvania Avenue station. (Columbia Historical Society)*

18

The tower of the B&O's New Jersey Avenue station, visible over the roof of the train platform, was imposing at first, but the city's build-up of surrounding land—undertaken in part to fight disease by covering over swamps— effectively dropped the depot into an earthen bowl above which the tower barely peeked. Patrons descended ramps and stairs to track level. The cars are wooden with open vestibules, and passengers contended with a snootful of locomotive smoke. Early coaches carried primitive coal stoves and a standard piece of Nineteenth Century cooling equipment: windows that opened. (Prints & Photographs Division, Library of Congress)

Switching sites did little to quell the railroad's racket in the halls of Congress, especially after the B&O stretched a spur across Pennsylvania Avenue through the Capitol's shadow, in hopes of connecting with southern lines at the Long Bridge on the Potomac. It took the Union Army to forge the link in 1861; until then, passengers had to tote their valises or jangle across the bridge in omnibuses to catch the Alexandria & Washington, a humble, six-mile line that connected with the Orange & Alexandria Railroad to the south. Come the Civil War, the Union Army moved throngs of soldiers south by rail across the Long Bridge into battle. In 1868 a writer perched on Capitol Hill would still find that "shrill screams of the engine[s would] frequently interfere with debate."

Awakened to the money to be made from a route into Washington, the B&O's arch-rival, the Pennsylvania Railroad, completed an end run, buying the rights to an obscure and dormant line, the "Baltimore and Potomac," to the tobacco towns of southern Maryland. Crafty Pennsylvania line agents had spotted a loophole in the railroad's charter that permitted construction of a spur up to 20 miles long anywhere on the main line. So the Pennsylvania set about snaking just such a branch from the town of Bowie in Maryland, across the Anacostia River, past the Washington Navy Yard, along "Dead Man's Curve" on Virginia Avenue, and into a new terminal. For that depot and train yard, Congress helpfully granted the new B&P 14 acres of public land on the Mall, hard by the city's sprawling Center Market.

The B&P station would earn a black mark for more than cinders and soot. In 1881, President James A. Garfield would be shot there by a demented office-seeker; a star on the floor marked the spot. During a particularly relentless Spring flood in 1889, the terminal's night matron, Alberta Shaughnessy (honored for her sharp eye in spotting "suspicious characters" like "Chicago Mae," a notorious diamond thief), would be observed rowing a boat across the depot's waiting room, scooping up carp.

B&O trains across the Avenue of the Presidents were bad enough. The clutter of Pennsy tracks, train sheds and huffing steam engines on what was supposed to be Pierre L'Enfant's sylvan Mall proved maddening. Twenty-seven evergreens planted along a ring of dirt that had been built as a sort of station blind had to be moved when it was discovered that locomotive smoke was killing them. So voracious were the railroads that the *Washington Star* suggested the Capitol itself as an ideal roundhouse. Despaired one U.S. senator, "In ten years' time there will not be a rod square of ground in all the Government reservations that is not occupied by a railroad depot with all its dirty surroundings."

In 1901, having just the year before toasted Washington's centennial with odes to its future as a "City Beautiful," a Senate commission charged with "improving parks" had had enough of raucous terminals, deadly grade crossings, and belching locomotives. It ordered the railroads back from the Mall, the B&O north, the Pennsy south. But the monumental urges of the nation's master architect and the clout of a captain of railroading would soon go that directive one better.

At the turn of the century Daniel H. Burnham looked, traveled, and daydreamed like the prosperous world architect that he was. Master of the epic World's Columbian Exposition in Chicago in 1893, he had helped uncork an American wellspring of Beaux Arts fervor. As architect of the regal Pennsylvania Railroad, Burnham had already chalked up a new Penn Station in Pittsburgh when he was invited to orchestrate the sweeping "Washington Plan," outfitting Washington in a colossal manner befitting a stripling world capital. The city lacked a memorial to Abraham Lincoln, sufficient executive-branch offices within hailing distance of the White House, a bridge from Virginia to L'Enfant's elm-lined Mall, and especially a plan to rid the Mall of its tawdry buildings and train tracks. Burnham promptly set off with other Senate park commissioners—colleagues all, from the Chicago world's fair—on a regal tour of European capitals. At the Piazza de Republicca two blocks from the Rome train station, he scribbled sketches of the Baths of Emperor Diocletian, the royal gym that had once featured (slave-driven) forced-air heat.

While the commissioners were off jaunting, the Pennsylvania Railroad was muscling control of the B&O. Why not, Burnham implored the Pennsylvania's president, Alexander Cassatt, whom he ran into in London, build a single "union station" that would give Washington back its unspoiled vistas, project the Pennsylvania's newfound hubris, and set the tone for the whole Washington Plan? For a federal payment of $3-million to offset construction costs of the tunnel under Capitol Hill needed to connect with southern lines, Cassatt agreed.

Left. *This is not Stanley or Livingston, a svelte William Howard Taft or Teddy Roosevelt without his glasses. It's America's master architect Daniel P. Burnham, whose epic, neoclassical Union Station was the first piece of the wholesale transformation of Washington from a swampy backwater town into a monumental world capital. (Union Station Redevelopment Corporation)*

Right. *This Burnham & Co. sketch highlights not only the grand scale of the massive terminal but also the architect's fondness for light, both natural—through a series of skylights—and manmade—via arc lights hidden in a balcony behind some of the stone sentinels who loom above what would later become a milling throng. The arc lights gave off a hideous blueish-white glare, which Burnham softened with yellow-tinted cathedral-glass screens. (Library of Congress)*

Below. *This fanciful vision of the Union Station grand plaza was inspired by the 1893 Columbian World's Exposition, which saluted the 400th anniversary, a year late, of Columbus's discovery of America. This aggrandized series of peristyles, reminiscent of the Place de la Concorde in Paris, was intended to pay proper homage to the United States Capitol. Neither the tightfisted railroads nor Congress would pay for such extravagance, however. (Library of Congress)*

Burnham's barrel-vaulted terminal would rise above the sewery remnants of Tiber Creek, on the edge of "Swampoodle," an infamous Irish shantytown. In *Mr. Lincoln's City*, Richard M. Lee wrote that the area had once been notorious for its "dirtiness, crime and dubious loyalty to the Union . . . the ideal place to turn a dishonest dollar." Residents kept goats amid decrepit buildings and the B&O coal yards. To construct his own Diocletian edifice beginning in October 1903, Burnham, whose "Make No Little Plans" credo would become architectural legend, brought in Italian labor gangs and lodged them in camp cars. The laborers patronized Irish stores and St. Aloysius Church but fought regularly with their neighbors. Before a single stone was in place, the workers spent a year building up the street grade and pouring concrete footings into the swampy soil. They spread close to 4 million cubic yards of fill dirt, enough to pack 80,000 hoppers stretching 600 miles, across the site. Gradually a bog 20 feet above mean tide was elevated to what *Building News* in 1908 called "an area of eminence" 60 feet above tide level over many acres. Taking together the construction of a massive terminal, plaza, tunnel under the Library of Congress, and trainyard complex and removal from the Washington cityscape of two sprawling railroad eyesores, the Union Station project was herculean. Observed Curator Robert Vogel at the Smithsonian Institution's Division of Engineering and Industry, "It was a whole lot more than the mere construction of a building where none had been."

The first granite slab was laid at the northeast corner of the station site in 1905. Architects, engineers, and inspectors dropped coins onto the mortar, where, the *Star* reported, they "will find an abiding place for many years to come." But the granite megaliths were strictly ornamental. A steel frame, encased in concrete for fire protection, bore the building's massive load. Into Union Station, Burnham built a central vacuum-cleaning system; crude cooling fans that blew air across revolving, brine-soaked burlap sheets; and a system of clocks synchronized from a master clock in the third-floor telegraph office. So immense were the new station's waiting room and concourse that a critic snorted, "Spring meets you at the train, and by the time you walk through to the exit, winter has come upon you."

The effect was properly pompous: Constantinian arches, egg-and-dart molding and sunstreaked gilt leafing, coffered ceilings and majestic skylights, delicate Pompeian traceries, towering statues by Louis Saint-Gaudens inside and out. The six 25-ton figures outside represented Prometheus and Thales (fire and electricity), Ceres and Archimedes (agriculture and mechanics), and Freedom and Imagination. Inside, behind the stone soldiers looming high above the Main Hall, Burnham hid huge arc lights, trained upward to produce a natural-light effect against the eggshell-white plaster ceiling. His Concourse immediately became the world's largest hall; it was said to be spacious enough to hold America's standing army (then 50,000 strong), or the Washington Monument laid flat. The building of 33 platforms and laying of 60 miles of track in the yards proceeded out back.

It's not hard to understand why McNulty Bros. rigged up a well-braced "moving scaffold"—or "traveler"—to complete both the gruelling construction of, and delicate finishing work on, Union Station's Main Hall ceiling from 1905 to 1907. Imagine the alternative: having to tear down and rebuild the scaffolding to reach each section along more than 220 feet of Roman barrel-vault ceiling, 90 feet high. The same moving-scaffold technique would be used again eight decades later, when the terminal got a facelift for its reopening as a transportation and shopping complex. (Prints & Photographs Division, Library of Congress)

Burnham designed rooms that over time would support a dining hall and lunch room; a "room set aside for the exclusive use of invalids"; a Presidential Suite later filled with furnishings of red leather, "priceless" rugs and crystal electroliers; a reading room; social hall; bowling alley; billiard parlor; sleeping quarters; railroad offices; tonsorial and shoeshine parlor — and even an upstairs space so long, the District of Columbia police department would rent it as a pistol range. The station featured not only "large and commodious" men's and women's toilet rooms, but also vast lounges for each gender. The men's anteroom became a smoking parlor, complete with the second-largest cigar stand in town.

Burnham commissioned the former president of Harvard University, Charles W. Eliot, to pick the inscriptions for the outdoor pavilions; Eliot would write several himself. The most familiar, because it is etched above the west carriageway, the only entrance most passengers would eventually be permitted to use, was a quote from Samuel Johnson:

HE THAT WOULD BRING HOME THE
WEALTH OF THE INDIES MUST CARRY
THE WEALTH OF THE INDIES WITH HIM
SO IT IS IN TRAVELLING – A MAN
MUST CARRY KNOWLEDGE WITH HIM
IF HE WOULD BRING HOME KNOWLEDGE

Eliot took it upon himself to comment on Saint-Gaudens' sculptures. "The necks all seem to me long in proportion to the length of the face, particularly Freedom's neck." Burnham soothed him by noting that long necks are essential to statuary that is viewed from 90 feet below.

A student from Pomona College in Claremont, California, Helmus Andrews, was asked by Saint-Gaudens to model for the interior legionnaires. Forty-seven years later, Andrews would visit the station for the first time. He pronounced the 46 final products "pretty crummy." If Eliot's criticisms of Saint-Gaudens' stonework could be ignored, those of the terminal's board of directors could not. "In blushing deference" to their female passengers, lest they take offense at the scantily attired soldiers, some of whom wore thigh-length tunic skirts and others nothing but a cape down their backsides, Saint-Gaudens was ordered to provide shields as modesty panels. Perhaps he protested that no more than a nebulous bump betrayed the guards' stony masculinity, but he complied.

True to the legacy of the Columbian Exposition, Burnham's plans called for a majestic plaza, ringed by peristyles and falling toward Pennsylvania Avenue along a new, diagonal avenue. The street would be built and tree-lined as Louisiana Avenue in the 1930s, but its sweeping rows of columns got no farther than the drafting board. In 1912 the plaza did receive Lorado Taft's ornate fountain and Old World/New World sculpture of Christopher Columbus. The ceremony would draw thousands of Knights of Columbus from across America, riding more than 100 special trains and jingling Washington Terminal Company cash registers.

A ghostly effect is noticeable under the station's Massachusetts Avenue arcade, looking west. The building facade is granite, but the materials under the arcade switch from granite to cheaper terra cotta and then plaster, the farther west one moves. Either the parsimonious railroads put a clamp on Daniel Burnham's free spending in mid-construction, or it was agreed going in that the President — whose suite was on the east end — would get granite and the masses could make do with faux materials. (Library of Congress)

Above. *Lenses were slow in 1908, a year after Union Station opened, when a photographer caught this view of the Concourse. It was a good thing passengers spent little time in the Concourse, for it was unheated and uncooled. Concourse lighting proved a difficult challenge. The skylight casts cheery light by day, but at night, lights trained upon the ceiling wash out any distinction between glasswork and ornamental plaster. (Library of Congress)*

Another Burnham brainstorm, that the plaza would be an ideal home to Lincoln's memorial, died a-glimmer. During World War I, a writer would observe that the area between the station plaza and the Capitol, where "temporary" dormitories for female government workers were rising, "leads only to weedgrown fields."

At 2:52 a.m. on Sunday, Oct. 27, 1907, the last train left the old B&O terminal, bound for Pittsburgh. Union Station's first train, from Pittsburgh, arrived the same morning at 6:50. Excitement abounded when B&O and Pennsylvania trains entered the yard together for the first time on November 17. For the station's formal opening almost a year later, veteran railroad employee H.P. Baldwin was permitted to buy the first ticket. It was photographed, and, a newspaper reported, presented to "Miss Kathryn Purnell, an Actress," who went to Baltimore.

Overleaf: *Wartime—when hale men were off at the front and women by the thousands filled civilian government jobs—is a recent memory in this photo, circa 1922. Female defense workers bunked in these hastily built "tempos" between the Capitol and Union Station where baseball diamonds had once sprawled. The first Senate office building, now called the Richard B. Russell Building, is on the right. (LeRoy O. King, Jr. Collection)*

29

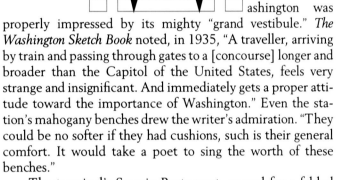

Washington was properly impressed by its mighty "grand vestibule." *The Washington Sketch Book* noted, in 1935, "A traveller, arriving by train and passing through gates to a [concourse] longer and broader than the Capitol of the United States, feels very strange and insignificant. And immediately gets a proper attitude toward the importance of Washington." Even the station's mahogany benches drew the writer's admiration. "They could be no softer if they had cushions, such is their general comfort. It would take a poet to sing the worth of these benches."

The terminal's Savarin Restaurant, named for a fabled Nineteenth Century French gourmet, served city eminents as well as train travelers. "Anybody who was anybody dined there," recalled Albert W. Browne in 1988. He had worked as a Pullman Co. porter in the 1920s. "Remember, people were traveling long distances; they wanted a fine dinner before they left." Because Union Station was the juncture between North and South and among seven passenger lines, customers had time to loll between connections, browsing through any of seven daily Washington newspapers. "The restaurant, the men's smoker, the whole atmosphere was refined, for the elite traveler," Browne continued." Why, the barber shop had 12 chairs and a bootblack and a valet to press your clothes." Ironically, former presidential adviser Charles A. Horsky remembered that the Savarin was "the only nice place in Washington you could dine with a black man."

The terminal was a magnet for the masses as well. "It was hot, plenty hot, in Washington in the summertime," said Browne. "But Union Station had those high ceilings. People would go inside just to cool off. It was a case of survival of the fittest!" Others remembered splashing, with an eye peeled for the terminal detective, in the Columbus Plaza fountain.

Left. *Well-heeled Washingtonians ate at Union Station's Savarin Restaurant whether or not they were traveling. Even train passengers had plenty of time for a leisurely meal or a dozen oysters at the Savarin's popular raw bar, because connecting time in Washington among seven passenger lines was often interminable. The terminal luncheonette was reached through the doors to the left, the kitchen to the rear. Some of the Savarin's fine china and sterling silver serving sets survived later trashings of this room; each is engraved with the terminal's intertwined WT logo. During World War II the restaurant switched hands, as the Union News Co. assumed the lease and converted the Savarin into the Gateway Restaurant. Blue-plate specials replaced fancy French meals. (Prints & Photographs Division, Library of Congress)*

Above. *At least one glistening taxicab was available at the terminal's West Portico in this 1920s photograph. East and west porte cocheres—carriage porches—were among the first designed for autos rather than horse-drawn phaetons. Tussles over a cab were commonplace at Union Station, as long-haul overnight sleepers emptied hundreds of travelers at a time. Pullman sleepers arriving in the middle of the night were switched to a side track, where their passengers could snooze until daybreak. Washington residents, who have long lived with a taxicab "zone" system, will recognize an anachronism on this cab: a meter. In fact, this vehicle was known as a "taximeter cabriolet." (Prints & Photographs Division, Library of Congress)*

Above. *The water was fine in the Columbus Plaza fountain in this circa-1926 shot. Some of the urchins who splashed there—not necessarily in this photo!—went on to work for the Washington Terminal Company in the considerably less blissful surroundings of the roundhouses or coach yards. (Union Station Venture, Inc.)*

Right. *Saint-Gaudens' statues, their stony masculinity discreetly secluded behind battle shields, overlook the Great Hall in this circa-1914 photo. The zealousness of early cleaning crews is apparent. (Graham, Anderson, Probst & White, Inc. Architects, Chicago)*

By 1928, 301 trains—one every five minutes—arrived or departed from the station each day. A *Star* reporter marveled as the K Tower controlled a Chinese puzzle of switches and semaphores and sent and received light-and-buzzer signals to and from conductors on the platforms just before trains pulled out. "There can be no napping or stopping to indulge in a little aside," he wrote. Holidays, inaugurations, and conventions especially taxed the trainmen. For the gathering of the Ancient Arabic Order of Nobles of the Mystic Shrine in June 1923, the Terminal figured it handled 6,000 extra pieces of baggage, 29,000 more gallons of milk in its restaurants and 200 extra tons of mail than it had for the 1921 Inaugural.

For the 1939 state visit of the King and Queen of England, the Terminal Company cut a special street to accommodate extra equipment, praetorian guards, and ceremonial trappings. More than 100,000 people packed the plaza to catch a glimpse of the royal couple. Foot traffic over the years ground down the waiting room floor—cupping the soft, white Vermont marble around its harder, red-marble "Champlain dots," causing "trips and stumbles." The marble would be replaced by sturdier terrazzo in 1951.

So crowded was the station in 1945 that Red Cap James (Doc) Carter would remember, 35 years later, "People used to bribe me to put them in wheelchairs so they could get to the trains in front of the crowds." Army Sgt. George Timko, who'd already been wounded in Germany, suffered a broken leg when he was trampled by a wartime holiday crowd. Writer E. L. Thompson observed, "The depot looks more like an army camp than a railroad station." In the U.S.O. lounge, hostess Anna Adams was moved to proclaim Union Station "the Crossroad of the World." The Terminal added a window to each ticket bay and built "Coach Only" and "Pullman Only" ticket booths in the middle of the floor. Out back, platforms had to be lengthened to handle longer trains. The *Washington Post* found "girl broadcasters" replacing time-honored male train-callers gone off to war, the women's "sweet voices having special appeal" to servicemen. No longer, wrote the paper, "does one see a leather-lunged train caller raise a battered megaphone to the general vicinity of his mouth and hear him voice the old familiar bellow:

"'Train leaving on Track 26 for Bal'more, P'burgh, Youngsto'n, Clevean', Dayton, Ind'nap'luss, Chiccago and all points westtt.'" The *Post* was flashing its poetic license, since Track 26 served long-haul trains to the Carolinas and points south.

Women wearing slacks, low-heeled shoes and "free and easy" clothing went to work cleaning coaches and even repairing 1,000-horsepower switching locomotives. They were taught two safety rules: "Don't stand on a rail, and don't stand in the middle of a track." Arriving passengers faced a battle-royal hailing a taxi. "Unaggressive people have been known to wait for an hour," wrote one onlooker. Diamond Cab's concession was described by the hackers' association president as "the most expensive in the world."

World War II, wrote Haynes Johnson in his 1980s novel *The Landing*, had transformed Union Station into "a pulsing nerve center . . . something more than a railroad station; now it, and the people who streamed through it, were part of an endless procession linked, inextricably, somehow, to the great release of raw energy that had been set in motion across the American continent."

Even in its later dotage, the terminal would feel isolated surges: Crusty railroad workers watched celebrants at the christening of the B&O's new streamliner, "The Cincinnatian," in 1947 "spill martinis down her sleek, blue sides." In 1963, more than 20 special trains, each carrying 1,000 people, streamed into Washington for the August civil rights march. Arriving passengers filled the Concourse with freedom songs; hundreds more would-be marchers were left behind for lack of room on trains. With those events and scant other exceptions, come war's end Union Station began a slide into soiled disuse, disrepair, and even disgrace.

Union Station was Washington's principal point of departure for soldiers and sailors heading off to basic training during World War II. The station's U.S.O. lounge affixed tags to sleeping servicemen so they could be awakened in time to catch their trains. This swabbie's girlfriend seems decidedly less enraptured than does the sailor in this greeting (or farewell) at the station. (Union Station Venture, Inc.)

THE HAUTE COUTURE
AND THE HOI POLLOI

To believe this promotional piece, the B&O's Capitol Limited had all the comforts of home. Competition was fierce between the B&O and Pennsy for the prime long-distance run, overnight to Chicago; the two railroads' premier trains west even left at the same time. Rival engineers would race each other out of the station, or at least appear to, to the delight of yard gangs. (John P. Hankey Collection)

Beggars and bedouin princes, Red Caps and red men, model railroaders and members of Congress have all mingled in Union Station's vaulted rooms: Lindbergh, Pickford, Khrushchev, Churchill, and squatters from the Community for Creative Nonviolence among them. For each, a story.

Workers once scaled one of the three flagpoles in front of the station to twist its gilded eagle to the right. Someone had complained that the eagle looked east, toward nondescript houses, rather than south, toward the source of inspiration and federal largesse, the U.S. Capitol. Thousands of mourners would huddle beneath those poles in 1945, awaiting the return of Franklin Roosevelt's body from Warm Springs. President Truman stopped by in 1951 to once again turn the Presidential Suite into a U.S.O. "V.I.P." installation "for just about the most important people of all," the men and women of the armed services. Mrs. Truman followed, days later, to cut another ribbon for a "Little Lounge—for Ladies." The facilities would revive a U.S.O. tradition: pinning colored labels to napping service personnel so wake-up calls would for sure be on time.

Once, in 1936, the Main Hall was cleared so 3,000 dignitaries from 54 nations could be fed at the World Power Conference. As a 28-piece orchestra serenaded from the balcony, the guests consumed 400 Virginia lambs, 9,000 select olives, a carload of broccoli, and 4,500 stalks of "choice celery placed at the right moment" before them. The *Star* marveled at "the delicate business of serving wines to foreign personages, and the delivery of ice cream before it melts away." Even at its seediest, days before it would be boarded shut as a safety hazard in 1981, Union Station would host an inaugural "Taste of America." *Post* food critic Phyllis Richman called it "a four-day snackathon" plied by 37 restaurants. Amid the fallen plaster and oily carpet stains, 100,000 celebrants wolfed down snails, fresh prawns, and zucchini curry soup.

When he was President, William Howard Taft was so portly he could not be comfortably seated in the Presidential Suite's modest wicker furnishings. Here, many years later and tens of pounds lighter, Taft is Chief Justice of the U.S. Supreme Court. Recovering from a hospital stay for a stomach ailment, he is wheeled to his train for a getaway to his Canadian fishing camp. Within a year, in February 1930, he would be further incapacitated by heart disease and forced to retire from the bench. Less than a month after that, on March 8, 1930, he would die at age 72. (Prints & Photographs Division, Library of Congress)

Right. *Units of the Army's First Division passed through Washington in September 1919, enroute from Germany, where they had fought and then served briefly as an army of occupation after Armistice Day. As Regular Army troops, they were not discharged from service but instead sent to Camp Taylor, Kentucky, for peacetime assignment to posts across the country. At this late-summer repast at Union Station, the doughboys and their guests got the watermelon, but it looks like the dandy in the bow tie got the girl. (Prints & Photographs Division, Library of Congress)*

Below. *Maybe it wasn't an uptown drawing room or Warwick's Billard Parlor, but the poolroom at Union Station's YMCA, maintained for railroad workers on the third floor of the terminal's East Wing, looks spiffy enough in this 1920 photograph. There's even a reading room in the back. The object that looks like a sink in the center doorway is a writing desk. Yardhands would send a fellow with 15¢ up to the Y, and he'd come back with a whole bucket of coffee. Poker games were not uncommon in these rooms, but, as befit a Christian establishment, tabs were kept and no money changed hands. (Dunlap Society Collection, Library of Congress)*

But ordinary folk became the stuff of anecdotes as well. In 1933, F.E. Prior observed overnight cleaning crews, "swinging along the smooth floor as if to the rhythm wrung out of a suds wagon and played on nine-foot mop handles." Night after night this "ceremonial dance of the cleaners is repeated," he wrote. "A long follow-thru and a relaxing swing as the long handle slips out its full length [and is] caught at the tip in the left hand while the scrubber's right foot is carried in a graceful arc over its mate." The crews' nemesis, another witching-hour visitor wrote, was chewing gum "firmly planted everywhere but in the waste-basket." The terminal's lost-and-found crew turned up umbrellas, army rifles, underwear, and false teeth. "Mr. Marshall, baggage-master, hopes that some day women will learn not to park rings and teeth in washrooms."

Privileged visitors got a peek at the "Metropolitan Southern Railroad," an elaborate model layout built in 1939 by area businessmen and enjoyed by off-duty train crews. Scenery depicted the landscape between Washington and Baltimore, "with a few western hills thrown in." To dispel any notion that their doings were kids' stuff or their creations toys, the rail club banned minors.

In 1934, *Post* writer Robert Cruise McManus found, besides an "antlike army" of station workers, "thirty thousand bankers, Gypsies, immigrants, Aunt Minnies, Senators, salesmen, football fans and funeral goers." He caught a basketball game at the YMCA gymnasium "up there somewhere" and watched huge "perambulators" thunder past, carrying pea soup for the lunchroom. Someone interviewed a ticket-taker, who reported the longest ticket sold to be a round-the-world voucher, paid for in cash. "Old cranks" remained a Red Cap's biggest headache, the dean of Union Station porters, John D. Sellers, lamented. "Women of the old school in particular, like creatures out of Dickens," asking innumerable questions. Sellers reported tips as meager as 15¢ by a Vanderbilt and as lavish as a dollar by an "average man." Henry Ford's tip, he added, was 35¢.

When baggage foreman George H. Thomas retired in 1953, he told of a day, prior to World War I, when he and his men turned the station inside-out, looking for two missing pieces of luggage. "I found them in what has always seemed to me the tragic nick of time," he told the *Post.* "In another hour or two their owner would have had to postpone his sailing for Europe—aboard the Lusitania." Station operations superintendent Paul Dowell retired in 1978, and he reminisced as well. He remembered a woman's barging into his office, demanding to be escorted to her husband's train compartment. "She said she was going to kill him," Dowell told the *Star,* "and sure enough, she pulled a gun out of her purse." The railroad official mollified her by explaining that, once purchased, a man's compartment is his castle, and "what happens once you're inside is your own private business." Yet another retirement, by the "Mayor of Union Station," manager Bernard R. Tolson, brought its own story. "A guy who said he just got out of the pen in New England popped in one day and summed up his assets," he said. "A little change, a railroad ticket to Colorado, and some clothing. He needed some traveling money. I gave him a little and told him to forget it. He did."

There were other incidents: • two boxcars, loaded with beer, uncoupling from a train at Takoma Park, rolling backward toward the staton; they smashed into a pillar and three parked coaches, and railroad crews labored through the night to slosh up the foamy debris • the 1961 walk-through of the station basement, its walls four feet thick; the cellar was intended by Burnham as a men's steam room and swimming pool but this day was eyed as a nuclear fallout shelter • the 1978 sit-in by the homeless, who spread foam mats and lugged in pots of coffee and food; eventually locked out, they dispersed into a bitter-cold night's air.

In 1942, the *Washington Times-Herald*'s Helen Essary had watched crowds of soldiers: "romantic-eyed dreamers made into fighting men against their wishes." But as Essary gazed outside the station and skyward, she would write, presciently, "The Magic Carpet is now the airplane. It awaits anybody with imagination."

Above. *General Haile Selassie bows to Mrs. Jacqueline Kennedy as President John F. Kennedy waits to greet the Ethopian emperor. It's not clear who presented whom with the roses. Union Station was the Washington arrival point of many dignitaries, some of whom, like Morocco's King Hassan, rode in style in elaborate private cars. (John F. Kennedy Memorial Library)*

Opposite. *Hundreds of homeless people, organized by the Community for Creative Nonviolence, "squatted" in Union Station over several winter nights in 1978, when the station was nearly dead as a passenger terminal and definitely dying as the National Visitor Center. The Department of the Interior tolerated the sit-in for several days but eventually evicted the contingent. (National Park Service)*

Railroad executives are a taciturn lot. So it is hardly surprising that bound minutes, some crumbling, from seven decades of Washington Terminal Company board of directors' meetings would be sparse and strictly business. Track layouts were changed, vendor leases negotiated, pensions approved, and matters like "applying power-operated reverse gear to W.T. engines 27 and 36" debated. But tucked in the faded mimeography are fleeting traces of the terminal's daily life:

1908. Machinists' wages rise to 32 cents an hour for a 10-hour day.

1909. The terminal defends several lawsuits involving locomotive smoke and vibration in neighborhoods fronting the First Street tunnel.

1910. The Board objects to purchasing upholstered furniture for the Presidential Suite. President James McCrea agrees that there should be some place to sit down but prefers that the suite be furnished "like a porch. We can't afford expensive furniture." The Board approves purchase of wicker and rattan for not more than $500. The railroads never did pay much attention to the suite. In 1939 government memoranda flew over the sorry state of the room where the British royal couple would be welcomed to Washington. Edward Bruce of the Treasury Department's procurement division wrote President Roosevelt that the suite "is very dingy with all the paint flaking off." The president approved spending $16,000 to paint the suite, cover "unsightly radiators," and replace "cheap-looking wicker."

1911. The Board complains of "considerable shrinkage" of ice between the American Ice Company plant and delivery and approves purchase of its own icemaking machine.

1912. The Anti-Saloon League claims that women and minors must pass the luncheonette bar, and that it is left unlocked on Sundays; the Board approves purchase of a wire enclosure. A megaphone system of train announcing is tested and found difficult to hear.

1913. At the death of Terminal Company president McCrea, a flag to drape in mourning is borrowed from the U.S. Capitol. The chairman suggests "it might be well for the Terminal Company to buy a flag for such purposes," but, true to McCrea's parsimony, no action is taken.

1914. The Board hears complaints that congressmen, diplomats and reporters are given the run of station platforms, but others without tickets are not permitted to see off friends and loved ones. The Board approves unlimited access to platforms—for a 10¢ fee.

1915. Placing benches in the Concourse is considered. The superintendent suggests deferring the project until Spring, as "very few people would care to sit in the Concourse during the winter weather."

1926. Board member H.W. Miller of Southern Railway "had recently experienced some annoyance when going north through Washington at night and again upon his return, by reason of loud talking in the station yards." The Board assigns a patrolman to "subdue noise in the vicinity of sleepers."

1931. Depression-time requests for rent reductions from the barber shop, bootblack, Savarin Restaurant, florist shop, and Western Union Telegraph Co. are begrudgingly granted. Entire meetings are devoted to "economies of operation."

Left. *It's a summer day at Union Station (the motorman is in shirt sleeves) in the 1920s, when the streetcar fare was a nickel. The lead streetcar is off to Georgetown via Pennsylvania Avenue. The second, like the first owned by the Capital Traction Company, has Connecticut Avenue as a destination. The third is an open car of the Washington Railway & Electric Company. One of Washington's most popular streetcar routes stretched from Union Station across town to American University and the Glen Echo amusement park. (LeRoy O. King, Jr. Collection)*

Above. *Terminal Company directors authorized a spacious Presidential Suite, but they turned penny-wise when the time came to furnish it. Since Presidents Garfield and McKinley had both been assassinated in railroad stations, Union Station executives wanted a secure, if sparse, place away from crowds. (Prints & Photographs Division, Library of Congress)*

51

1936. Following complaints from the Fine Arts Commission "relative to the grime which has blackened the statues and architecture of the Station," the Board orders cleaning of "the more noticeable features."

1941. The Board gets no response from the Fine Arts Commission on a proposal to install a marquee in front of the Station. The signboard would later be approved as an information service to wartime crowds but would be ordered down at war's end.

1943. Alcoholic beverages are removed from the station drug store "to cut down on intoxication in trains." Sales would resume four years later "in view of the cessation of hostilities . . . as well as on account of the additional revenue to be derived."

1950. The decline in daily ticket revenue and movement of cars begins to show in Board records. From $80,000 and 3,753 cars and engines in 1945, the daily average had dropped to $34,000 and 2,966 cars. By 1963, when the figures would last be noted, they would fall below $22,000 and 1,600 cars a day.

1951. As troops again mass at Union Station for trips to Korean War marshaling points, the Board gives "sympathetic consideration" to a request to install a billboard "for the purpose of displaying messages of spiritual guidance" but turns it down as "an undesirable precedent."

1952. The notion of appointing a p.r. person is rejected, the Board feeling that the Terminal Company "enjoys excellent public relations" already.

1956. Severe cost-cutting measures include replacing cloth towels with electric hand dryers, installing parking meters, supplanting several Red Caps with luggage carts, closing the employees' Ivy City lunchroom, and eliminating brakemen from many crews.

1959. The Board authorizes $2,873 to install a 1,000-ft. bird barrier to prevent roosting in the West Portico.

1964. The station's soda fountain is "retired," replaced by soft-drink machines.

1975. Board minutes grow scant. A suspension of construction of the National Visitor Center, due to a strike, is noted.

1978. The terminal manager notifies the Board that the National Visitor Center has shut more than half the Concourse, closed numerous offices, and evicted the Terminal YMCA "in order to save on the cost of heat."

1981. The Board is informed that "all Department of the Interior employees have left [the remnants of the visitor center] . . . except for two or three people."

There would be little else beyond gloomy auditing reports before the terminal fell to the control of a new, nonprofit corporation charged with resuscitating the grande dame of rail transportation.

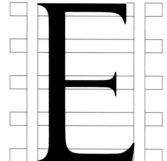

A car repairman — or "car knocker" — works his cigarette to the nubbin during a break in the 1930s or '40s. The work of the "bull gangs" in the shops of Union Station was hard and modestly rewarded, but the men were thankful for it. It included everything from hefting ponderous cars off their wheels to loading 30 to 40 huge blocks of ice into compartments under each coach. Cold water from the melting ice was circulated through a tube in the air-handling duct in the passenger compartment. The effect was modestly chilling at best, and many trains remained uncooled at all, well into the 1960s. The commotion of the Union Station yards prompted the owner of neighboring Uline Arena, which served as a temporary troop hostel during World War II, to brick in its windows against the racket, so the men could sleep. (Union Station Venture, Inc.)

Even in thriving times, most Washington Terminal Company employees were invisible to the public. They held musclepower "bull jobs" in the basement baggage room, locomotive shop or coach-repair yard. The five men who sat in the station manager's office in 1988, spinning memories, averaged 47 years in such jobs.

When supervisor Elton Miller was first hired, he would think back later, "a man told me, 'Never rains on the railroad, and furnish your own work clothes.' That meant, 'You come to work, don't make any diff'rence. We expect you to be here.'" Besides the 22 daily trains to Philadelphia; the 14-coach New York trains; the 18-car Florida Specials; he re-called the "crack trains" to the west: the B&O's Capitol Limited and Pennsy's Liberty Limited. Both left each after-noon at 5:30. "When they got to New York Avenue, one would go that way, one would go t'other," Miller said. "It was like the engineers'd race each other coming out."

Shoulder-high sacks, tagged, "Working Mail," were tossed onto each train. "Clerks'd sort it on the way, county by county," Miller said. "They'd make up bags and drop 'em, and mail catchers'd pick up more at each stop." The yards would be full of sleeper cars. "The first one pulled in here, 3 o'clock in the morning," Miller recounted. "We'd pull 'em off and set them on their own track. People would sleep in the station [yard] all night long. One track was 10, 15 Pullman cars from different trains." The ritual worked in reverse each evening. "We called it 'nightlining.' You'd get on the train at 8:30 at night and go on to bed. The trains left at 2 in the morning."

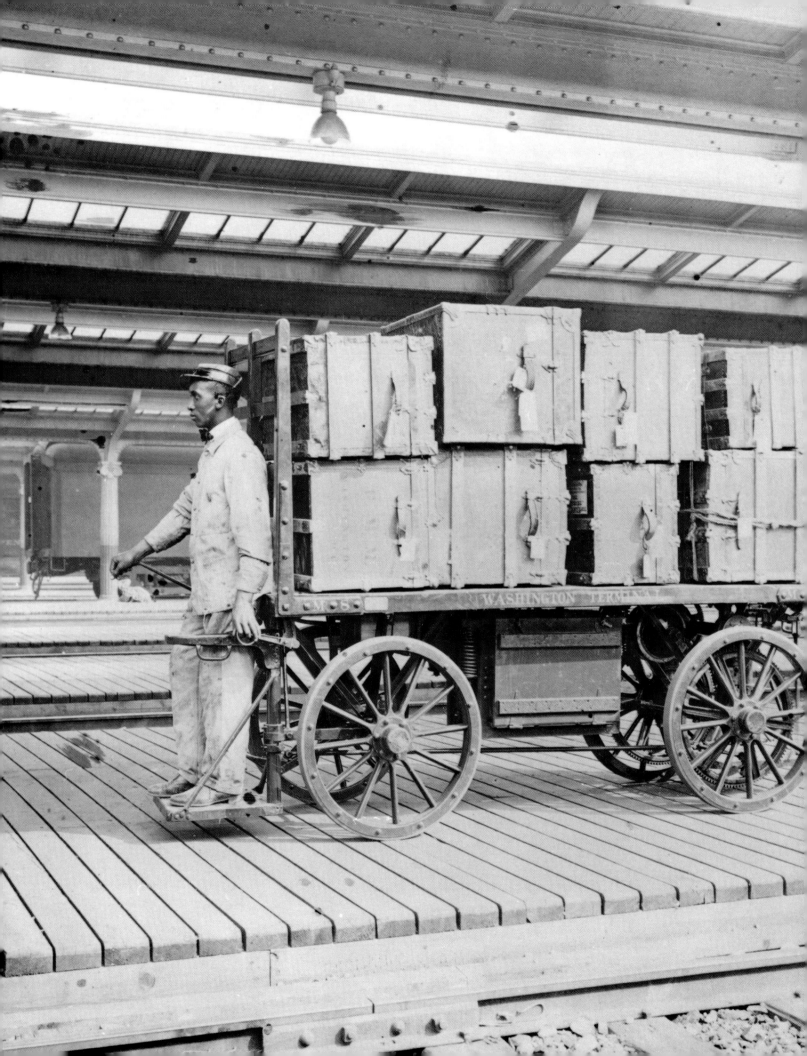

The railroaders loved the old steam locomotives. "Them engineers'd wear a kerchief, goggles on, pants tied at the bottom" said Miller. They had their own living quarters in the engine house, cooked their own meals on an old stone stove. To see ahead, engineers had to stick their heads out the window. "They'd come out the other end of the tunnel, black with soot, and keep right on goin'." Machinist Frank DiMeglio said of the steam engineers, "They'd come out four hours before startin' time, polishing the railings, the bells, oilin' somethin'." To the Terminal bulls, engineers were all "Cap": "How you doin', Cap?"

Each engine had a personality. Mechanics could tell which engineer was running which locomotive by the engine and steam-whistle sounds: "You could tell it was Number 34, and Old Man Brown was running it." The clattery engines kept a huge crew busy at the Ivy City turntable—the spokes of tracks in the maintenance roundhouse. "Every hun'erd miles or so, they'd shake themselves loose: bolts, nuts, fittings," DiMeglio recalled. "Steam engine'd go through those mountains, chuggin' and bouncin' and a-slappin', the bushings'd burn up."

DeMeglio weighed 115 pounds when he started, he said. "Big boilermakers, big rawboned rascals, they'd boot you around." Foremen were the law in the yards. "If you talked to 'em, it was 'Yes, sir,' 'No, sir.' You wouldn't dare suggest anything. You were late? You were gone; they'd fill that job on the spot. Hell, one man would control 300 trains goin' out. You had to admire 'em. Now, hell, I don't see nothing *but* foremans." Elton Miller remembered a foreman named "Big Ed." "He'd walk through the roundhouse, people'd scatter." If a mechanic messed up a repair job, he'd sneak out back, bury the part, and start over: better that than face the foreman. DiMeglio said new hires quickly learned the ropes, or else. "I 'member a machinist told me one time, 'Go get an Old Man.' I went out there and got the old man from the toolroom. He said, 'goddamn it, that ain't the Old Man.' There's a jig you bolt down to drill some holes. *That* was the Old Man."

General foreman Vincent J. Tana started as a car cleaner. "Water'd freeze right on ya," he said, "but you kept goin'. You were grateful for the job. We'd take firebuckets and barrels, put packin' in 'em [and set them on fire] to keep warm. My paycheck for two weeks, seven days a week, averaged 55 dollars. I thought I was a millionaire." Tana would sometimes assist a pipefitter, repairing plumbing at the Savarin Restaurant. "'Course I couldn't afford to go in there. Meal'd run ya six bucks. It was outta my league. The chef'd slip ya a chicken leg or somethin'. That was high livin'."

The men remembered Christmases: mail pouches stacked high in Concourse corners, the Main Hall so crowded, "you'd trip over somebody just stretchin' to hear the carols." "Bill Norman, one of the supervisors, 'd play the organ," said Tana. "Ever'body was in a fine mood." Trains would run in two or three sections, each with its own flag whipping past the K Tower. Passengers arrived two or three hours early to be sure of a seat.

Opposite. A baggage porter rattles down a platform on a battery-powered electric baggage cart. This was the very early days of Union Station, since the platforms were soon paved with cement. Given the shutter speed of the times, the porter was actually posing, rigidly still. Steamer trunks were common in the early years of this century. Salesmen traveled with samples, and well-heeled passengers began a transatlantic shipping cruise with a train ride to New York or Baltimore. A 1908 B&O Railroad pamphlet extolled the station's umbrella sheds, where "there is never an accumulation of smoke, steam or gasses to annoy the passengers." (Prints & Photographs Division, Library of Congress)

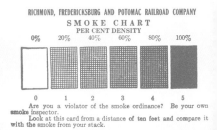

RICHMOND, FREDERICKSBURG AND POTOMAC RAILROAD COMPANY
SMOKE CHART
PER CENT DENSITY

0%	20%	40%	60%	80%	100%
0	1	2	3	4	5

Are you a violator of the smoke ordinance? Be your own smoke inspector.
Look at this card from a distance of ten feet and compare it with the smoke from your stack.

Above. Rookie switcher firemen held up this pocket-sized chart, Picassolike, to help them guage the quality of the burn when they fired a locomotive's coal furnace. Any reading of 4 or greater put them in jeopardy of an inspector's reprimand. Firemen had an especially difficult time meeting smoke-quality standards during World War II, when high-grade coal was diverted to the military. The draft of a moving locomotive kept coal in boilers burning thoroughly. But when the train was stationary, the fireman had to activate a blower and keep his firebox door ajar. (William R. Hutson Collection)

Above. *This was a train's worth of mail moving through Union Station to the U.S. Post Office next door. It must have been a valuable shipment; note the shotgun tucked under the attendant's arm. During a spate of banditry in the 1920s, U.S. Marines rode mail cars as sentries. At Christmastime, mail sacks were stacked near to the Concourse ceiling. Mail going the other direction, onto trains, was sorted enroute and tossed off onto platforms across America. It was soon after railroads began losing lucrative mail business to airplanes that passenger service began to decline. (Prints & Photographs Division, Library of Congress)*

Right. *This ticket's owner must have been both frugal and fussy. Scrawlings on other pages of this voucher show $1.70 later refunded from the $174.57 round-trip double fare. (John P. Hankey Collection)*

Foreman Lawrence Heffner said "ever'body had their own [yard] whistles. They'd want somebody, they'd blow his whistle." The Pennsylvania and B&O had distinctive calls. Terminal Company foremen had theirs, usually two longs and a short, and there was the universal "trouble whistle." When you heard it, everything stopped. On New Year's Eve at midnight, every whistle in the yard, and on every train, would sound. "You could hear 'em five miles away," said Tana.

Carman Jim Snyder enjoyed working the "wreck trains" that would sally as far as Brunswick, Maryland; and he loved the company's sports: bowling, playing pool, watching fighters train at the Terminal YMCA gym. "We had a ball league, strictly railroad. We'd play at 21st and Constitution Avenue. One time I slid into third, looked up, and there's President Truman, noddin' his head, FBI men about a block away. He wouldn't walk with 'em. I nodded my head, he nodded his and went on down the road."

The men worked on the Ferdinand Magellan, the bulletproofed Presidential private car. They built a special lift for the crippled F.D.R., replaced bathroom windows an inch thick, cleaned and draped the train for Dwight D. Eisenhower's funeral ("Sure that wasn't *Lincoln's* funeral, Vince?" Heffner cackled), gussied up Mrs. Johnson's "Lady Bird Special." They remembered laying the red carpet alongside Track 18, down which John F. Kennedy walked to greet King Hassan of Morocco at his rococo private car. But Harry Truman was their favorite. Recalled Tana, "His daughter Margaret would go up to New York to take music lessons, and she'd always come back Friday night. Either Harry or Bess or both of 'em'd be there at the station, waiting for Train 175. Mr. Truman'd look at his watch and tell me, 'Son, that train's runnin' a little late.' 'Yup,' I'd say. Here he was, the President, and he and Bess'd be out there every week to meet her."

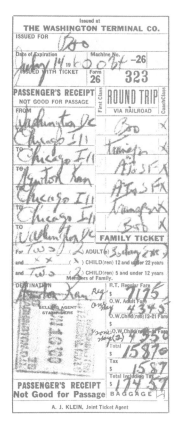

There were lavish private cars: Anheuser Busch's Number 10,000: the "Adolphus"; U.S. Steel Co.'s stainless-steel-top, red-bottom "Fairless"; President Roosevelt's first car, the "Savannah"; the Southern's fleet, brought up for Terminal Company board meetings. And there were the "specials": hundreds of trains for each inauguration, schoolkid excursions from West Palm Beach; Democratic and Republican specials to the Greenbriar, W.Va., spas; 25 trains to the Army-Navy football game in Philadelphia; and, as late as the 1980s, a seven-car "White Snake Special" for a rock group, arranged by the MTV cable network.

Railroads' heyday was warmly recalled, all right: pork dinners with the chef on dining cars, a fresh bass cooked at Seaboard Air Line's own diner out back, platforms full of kazoo-tooting Shriners. (The Seaboard Air Line was a railroad, a predecessor of the Seaboard Coast Line.) But there were lean times, too. During the Depression, recalled DiMeglio, "We'd get about 86 cent an hour, minus 10 percent. They'd take that out for the Terminal Comp'ny, to keep it goin'. You'd work 365 days a year. Take a couple days off, they'd fire you." During passenger railroads' decline in the 1960s, Lawrence Heffner remembered, "them New Haven cars'd come in with broke windows. They'd put on a sign, 'Vandalism.' But that don't fix the glass. We'd just send 'em back out like they was."

Mostly, though, the work was honest, satisfying. Said Frank DiMeglio, "We'd really roll them engines out."

Below. Red Cap William Druitt grabs a break alongside Track 15 in 1957. The professional porter was an indispensable part of train travel. You'd want a Red Cap, even if you were carrying a single, light case, since wily porters knew every trick to securing a cab. The Washington Terminal Company once tried banning the tipping of Red Caps, substituting instead a flat fee of 10¢. Many passengers ignored the regulation, however, preferring the personalized service of a wise entrepreneur. (Washingtoniana Division, D.C. Public Library)

"RUN FOR YOUR LIVES!": THE WRECK OF THE FEDERAL EXPRESS

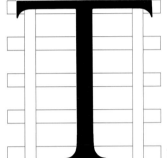

Thursday, January 15, 1953 had dawned cloudy and unseasonably mild as Train 173, the Pennsylvania Railroad's crack Federal Express, gobbled its last taste of speed. Churning 18 minutes late and clipping 80 on the owl run from Boston, Pennsy's GG-1 electric engine No. 4876 and 16 silver coaches pounded onto the first switching tracks into Washington at Landover, Maryland, two miles from Union Station.

The streamliner's manifest listed 400 or so coach and sleeping-car passengers, including an early wave of Republican celebrants, come to see General Dwight D. Eisenhower inaugurated five days hence. Many passengers had already heaved down their bags and were sidling toward the front of the train for a quick getaway at the gate.

Passing Landover, 66-year-old engineer Henry W. Brower tugged firmly on the air-brake lever. It was an autonomic routine he had performed thousands of times over a long railroading career. The 1,200-ton juggernaut shuddered and reined effortlessly to 60 m.p.h., then, less than a mile later after another nudge, down to 50.

It was 8:30 a.m., six minutes to disaster.

At the Ninth Street overpass, Brower again coaxed the brake. This time, the train hiccupped but did not slow down. Adrenaline instantly coursing, the engineer wasted no time pondering. He rammed the brake to "Full Emergency" for what should have been a squealing panic stop well short of the terminal.

The Federal never paused. It was time to sound the trainman's desperate, staccato, "Runaway!" call.

Engineer Russell Edelin guides a terminal steam switching locomotive in 1943. Ten years later, another engineer, Henry Brower, would be battling to control an entirely different kind of engine—the giant electric GG–1. Brower could see perfectly well what was coming, for the runaway GG–1 had front windows. (J.E. Pierson/William R. Hutson Collection)

63

Whistle shrieking, she cannonballed past the C Tower and then K Tower, where signalman John Feeney had routinely aligned Track 16 for her arrival. Stunned to see the train run amok, Feeney frantically considered shunting 173 onto spur tracks. But these were still flush times; adjacent tracks were full.

Too late, anyway. Four city blocks from the terminal and doing 40, the Federal barreled into the one-degree decline toward the station. Feeney grabbed the direct line to the stationmaster's office. "Runaway on 16!" he shouted to clerk Ray Klopp, who blanched to see the Federal "not more than three or four carlengths" away and bearing down. Klopp leaped from his chair, scattering clipboards, and screamed to four other clerks, "Run for your lives!"

Aboard, passengers formed a freeze-frame of terror. Some clutched the closest soft object: a pillow, a laundry bag, or each other. As the express charged past the Ivy City roundhouse, a woman screamed. Conductor T.J. Murphy bounced from car to car. "Get down on the floor! Lie down in your seat!" he hollered.

Dead ahead, frantic alarms had cleared the Concourse. As the monster locomotive slammed into Track 16's end bumper, obliterating it, station clerk Klopp was reaching to dial the rescue services that would surely be needed. After annihilating the rear platform, the engine reared upward like an enraged mustang, burst with a shower of sparks and dust through the stationmaster's shed and station wall, and flopped into the Concourse. The runaway pulverized a concrete stanchion and what an instant before had been the newly expanded Union News Co. stand. "I thought somebody had tossed a bomb at one of the trains," said Senator Herman Walker of Idaho, on hand to greet his state's former governor.

It was 8:36 a.m. The time is known because the stationmaster's clock was found crumpled and welded on that moment.

With a bellow, the thick concrete floor collapsed under the engine's 230 tons of deadweight, and Engine 4876 and two lead coaches zig-zagged into the basement. Four workers in the mammoth baggage room there were trapped briefly, but all survived. Dozens of baggage and mail workers would normally have been posted directly below the 8,000-sq.-ft. crater torn by the falling behemoth. Instead, they were on a fortuitous coffee break.

The third coach settled on a cant at the lip of the hideous hole. Four other cars derailed just outside. Nearby Pennsy employees, Traveler's Aid nurses, and ordinary citizens quickly jumped, or smashed their way, aboard the train to search out the injured. A passenger shattered the smoker-car window with a chair. "I've always wanted to do that!" he exclaimed. There was no fire, just the sizzle of severed brake lines and downed wires.

Somehow, no one was killed; only 43 people required hospitalization. Girded to pry mangled bodies from beneath the engine and sunken coaches, rescuers instead found none. The engineer and brakeman were led, dazed, from their cab. Neither said a word.

The Concourse was soon a maelstrom of red lights, stretchers, and ambulances. Raymond Klopp and other trainmen got busy heeding the call to "get all the morphine you can" from Union Station's drugstore. D.C. Fire Department pumpers not already fighting another fire, at a tire shop fire 10 blocks away, burst straight into the Concourse and trained their hoses on the crippled engine below. But the GG-1's batteries did not explode; its spilled transformer oil did not ignite.

Thirty-four years later, in retirement in Rockville, Maryland, Train 173 passenger Edward K. "Bud" Koch flashed back to the horror "like it just happened." He had been inbound from his home in Baltimore to his job as a design artist. As a "regular," Koch knew the ordinary, lulling sounds of a comfortably decelerating train. "I realized we had trouble when we hit a switch at what seemed like left angles," he recalled. "We were doin' 40 at least, and we weren't slowing down. Joe [a crew member] came runnin' through, told us to brace ourselves. Some people were screaming, but mostly there wasn't time to do much reacting.

"It's funny, but I don't remember much of a noise when it hit. Screeching metal, but no big 'boom.' What I remember was the cloud of concrete dust. That train just tore through the platform like butter, literally powdered it.

"I ended up on the floor, but I remember seeing something out the window that I'll never forget. In the middle of the dust and the sparks from the electric wires that had been knocked down, I watched, just like it was in slow motion: The undercarriage of one of the cars flew up in the air and came down right next to our car. I don't know to this day how no one was killed."

Reports of the calamity spread quickly. But inquisitive locals and inaugural visitors, including 32 full-blooded Arizona Indians in feathered headwear, were surprised, and maybe disappointed, to arrive and find the wreck ingeniously camouflaged within two days of the crash. The shredded stationmaster's office and newsstand were replaced in a whisk, the gaping Concourse hole repaved, even the mangled iron grillwork at the point of entry replaced and freshly painted. Using 400 men 'round the clock, "We had the job licked in 36 hours," said Terminal Manager Sidney Kerl. Track 16 was back in service within three days.

Even as, a mile away, Ike was swearing to uphold the Constitution as President, Washington Terminal wreckmaster Frank Swofford's crews were cutting what was left of the $750,000 engine into six giant hunks. News accounts stated that 4876 had been sold for scrap, its dials and wires cannibalized. Not so. On orders of Pennsy's insurer, Lloyd's of London, the GG-1 was hauled to the company's Altoona, Pennsylvania, shops, nimbly reassembled, and returned to service. Amtrak later sold 4876 to a New Jersey commuter line, for which it ran until it was mothballed in 1979.

An Interstate Commerce Commission inquiry, convened nine days after the wreck, absolved the train crew; indeed, their bravery was commended. Discounting whispers of sabotage, the commission laid the accident to a frozen "angle cock valve" in the third coach's air-brake system.

Bud Koch, who had been riding directly above the faulty valve, would be forced to wear a back brace and girdle for more than a year. "I was a bit of a celebrity," he said. "For a long time, people on the train from Baltimore would joke whether, this time, it was going to stop. One fellow laughed and said, 'If they're gonna go *through* the station, they might as well keep on goin' and take me to work.'

"I didn't think it was too funny at the time."

AN AGING LADY

In this late-1940s photo, crews appear to be getting the upper hand on some of the grime that autos, steam locomotives, and the passage of time had wrought. How much snappier is the stone figure to the right than its blackened neighbor. (Prints & Photographs Division, Library of Congress)

In 1948 Americans logged 44 million passenger miles on trains and airplanes. Eighty percent took the train. Nineteen years later, the ratio had more than reversed: 88 percent preferred to fly. Across the landscape, work crews laid runways and wide, fast highways. Railroads, for whom passenger service had been a break-even proposition at best, pruned rolling stock, slashed schedules, and gutted or leveled sepulchral stations.

Southern Railway's chief executive officer, Graham Claytor, oversaw that line's gutting of passenger service. Later, as Amtrak's president, he remembered, "The secondary trains had to go, and they went. We unloaded all of our passenger stations as quick as we could. If you're in the freight railroad business, why in God's green earth do you want a mausoleum for a passenger station. All it does is cause trouble, so you get rid of it, quick as you can."

As they retrenched, railroads cried "foul" about their tax disadvantages. Noted *Railway Age* in 1951, "Union Station in Washington, D.C. . . . cost the railroads $21 million back in 1907; on it, they pay, in addition to all operating expenses and interest, about $290,000 per year in property taxes. . . . By contrast, the railroads' air line competitors use a tax-free Washington airport built entirely at government expense, [and] yet the air lines pay only nominal charges of a few thousand dollars a year for its use."

As late as 1961, as architectural historian Frederick Gutheim was calling business at Union Station "a ghost of its former self," the terminal was the highest-taxed commercial structure in Washington. Union Station "is a lonely place these days," rued Gutheim. Contemporaries called it "a quiet catacomb" and a "depressing cavern where people no longer come," looked upon by the railroads as "a costly nuisance to be treated with neglect."

Latter-day Union Station would not see many crowds to match this exuberant gathering that welcomed home the Washington Senators from a successful western trip in which the "Nats" won 9 of 10 games in May 1949. Baseball considered Detroit, Chicago and St. Louis "west" in those days. The giddy swing moved the Senators into the rarified first division — the top four teams of what was then the eight-team American League. "We can do it," reads one of the signs, referring to hopes for the first Washington pennant in 16 years. But the team quickly reverted to form, finishing last with a 50–104 record. The open car awaits four Senators' officials for a motorcade to the White House. Eynon was team secretary, Wolff the Senators' broadcaster, Bluege the manager, and Griffith the longtime owner who eventually moved the team to Minneapolis-St. Paul. (Washingtoniana Division, D.C. Public Library)

By 1958, the B&O and Pennsylvania roads were talking about giving Union Station away. Pennsy President James M. Symes told Senate hearings on "the problems of railroads," "If we could donate the Washington terminal property, which is the Union Station, to the Government, and if the Government permitted use in the same manner as the airport to us," Symes reasoned, "the owners would accrue about $5 million in cash and save well over a million dollars a year in operating expense."

But the railroads had a fallback position. They were quietly costing out plans to tear down the monolithic station and throw up an office building. Architect Seymour Auerbach, who conducted such a study, remembered many years later that it was clear that the terminal could not continue as a full-fledged train station. "It would be like taking the Cathedral of Seville," he said, "and making it the church of a 150-person village." "The railroads had a developer in New York City ready to go," remembered Knox Banner, who headed a business group, Downtown Progress, that as early as 1963 proposed turning Burnham's mighty structure into a visitor and student center. One scheme for a national cultural center—what would become the Kennedy Center for the Performing Arts—suggested turning Union Station into a concert hall. In 1965, a Smithsonian Institution study concluded that Union Station would make a fine railroad museum. But Smithsonian Secretary S. Dillon Ripley passed, noting that other projects, especially an air-and-space museum, took priority.

A passenger creates his own seat in this 1957 photograph. Station lockers, visible behind him, were one of many meager efforts by the Washington Terminal Company to make a buck in the face of rapidly declining traffic. Soda machines between gates were another. Long gone are the station's drug store, restaurant, and sparkling-clean luncheonette. The lockers would later be removed—the last in 1986—in the nervous days of worldwide terrorism that would come. (Washingtoniana Division, D.C. Public Library)

Gaudy plastic seats, thought to be a "modern" improvement and designed to outfox transient sleepers, were bolted to the terminal floor in 1967. They, and push-it-yourself luggage carts, gave the station the look of a small-town bus station; by that time, it had a volume of traffic to match. Yard crews showed up for work one day and found Union Station's solid, old mahogany benches piled high at the depot's dump. (Washingtoniana Division, D.C. Public Library)

The railroads would "dearly love to replace Union Station with a sleek, profitable office colossus as they would like to replace their remaining passenger trains with sleek, profitable freight trains," wrote *Post* architectural critic Wolf Von Eckardt. "Vague daydreaming about what a lovely auditorium or visitor center Union Station might make will not redress the station's red balance sheets, [and] you can't run a railroad on sentiment." Union Station's barons of the bottom line were as arrogant, Von Eckardt wrote, "as the white lions flanking the Columbus fountain in front of it, which stick their marble noses high in the air."

But it would not be so easy for the railroads to raze Union Station to build an office tower, as the Pennsylvania did its storied New York station in 1966. Although the "preservationist movement" was five or more years from full flower, a quasi-official committee chaired by Washington architect Francis Lethbridge had, two years earlier, declared Union Station one of 20 buildings in Washington deserving of "category one" landmark status, meaning that "it must be preserved." The designation packed no force whatsoever, other than intense suasion on owners doing business a cinder's throw from Congress. Still, it was clear that *something* had to be done soon. When he closed the Union News stand in the station concourse in 1968 and retired, 46-year-veteran Earl Stanley Jones told the *Star*, "The station's like a tomb."

71

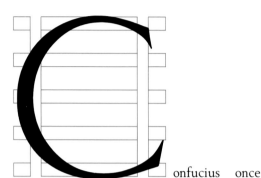

Confucius once said, "Things that are done, it is needless to speak about. Things that are past, it is needless to blame." But sagacity did not stop just about everyone who had a hand in Union Station's forlorn "National Visitor Center" incarnation from blaming someone else for what went wrong. Terribly wrong.

The notion that Daniel Burnham's museum piece might make a dandy visitor center gained momentum as soon as passenger-rail traffic dropped off. The National Park Service, which had long sought a showcase for Smokey the Bear's city cousins, calculated there were 10,000 visitors descending on Washington each day, and members of Congress heard the yowls of their constituents who scrambled for the Mall's few parking spaces, only to run afowl of zealous meter-readers and gypsy towtrucks.

Although it was far from the tourist action of the Mall and lay in a marginal neighborhood—no longer Swampoodle but certainly not chic—Union Station seemed a logical place for an orientation center. It sat at the throat of a likely through-city superhighway; who could know that only a stub of a road would ever be built? Union Station was set to get one of the city's first subway stops, had plenty of space above its train tracks to park buses and cars, and seemed an ideal spot to store and dispatch "interpretive shuttle" jitneys called Tour-mobiles. In 1965, Federal Aviation Administrator Najeeb Halaby even suggested that the site could accommodate helicopters and short-takeoff, steep-climbing air-shuttle jets to New York, barreling down a runway paved over the railway marshalling yards. Although that idea never took wing, the notion of turning the old station into a "multi-modal" transportation complex became central to several plans. After all, one of the city's most popular streetcar lines had traversed the city from Union Station to American University and the Glen Echo amusement park.

Architect Seymour Auerbach's plan for the National Visitor Center shows a hole in the Main Hall floor, but it was nothing like the walled-in "Pit" that would actually be built. His model envisions a plethora of lower-level visitor activities, including movies and an illuminated map of the Washington area to help orient tourists. What the Department of the Interior constructed, instead, was a slide show in a box canyon. (Seymour Auerbach)

Inconveniences to passengers that were "deeply regretted" as Union Station was converted to the National Visitor Center were nothing compared with the Department of the Interior's later regrets at having begun the center at all. The inconveniences of this time paled beside those that lay ahead, as passengers would be directed along twisted paths toward a distant train. This cozy Christmastime tableau would be the last good cheer at Union Station for many years. A huge Pit would soon occupy much of the floor in this scene. (Washingtoniana Division, D.C. Public Library)

For the Nation's Bicentennial observance historic Union Station is being converted to the National Visitor Center...

"Any inconvenience caused the traveling public during this conversion is deeply regretted"

Ronald H. Walker
Director, National Park Service

Rogers C.B. Morton
Secretary of the Interior

NATIONAL VISITOR CENTER

A starry vision crystallized in 1967 when John W. Macy, Jr., chairman of the U.S. Civil Service Commission, foresaw Union Station as a locus of America's approaching Bicentennial, "monumental enough to meet the needs of what will certainly be a gigantic birthday party that will attract millions of guests." For the party, Macy even proposed moving "our sacred documents" into the building.

Interior Secretary Stewart L. Udall was a believer. He wrote Macy that the center should indeed be planned on a "grand scale." "In the guise of seeing whether Union Station could be a railroad museum, we managed to put together a study commission to show it could be a visitors' center, which is what Udall thought would be an alternative that might fly," remembered Charles Horsky, then adviser to President Johnson for District of Columbia affairs. The committee report quoted Vice President Humphrey as taking up the cudgel for tourists: "The time passed generations ago for us in Washington to meet our common obligations to common courtesy." Union Station would be just the place to "enrich the visitor's own objectives in ways he might not have been prepared to expect," the Udall commission report agreed. The visitor's experiences would turn out to be unexpected, all right.

Enter Rep. Kenneth J. Gray of downstate Illinois, who, when the visitor center became the National Fiasco, would be remembered in the *Post* as a "former auctioneer and used-car salesman." Gray chaired the House subcommitee on public buildings and grounds, and he helped work out a deal that, he would become infamous for saying, "won't cost the taxpayers a penny." Years later Gray would take pains to point out that Thomas S. Kleppe, the man who as Gerald Ford's Interior Secretary would make the first move that killed the visitor center by stopping work on its parking garage, had cosponsored the enabling legislation as a congressman.

Under the 1968 deal, Union Station's railroad owners would borrow $16 million to reconfigure the gargantuan building as a visitor center: $5 million for renovation, $11 million to construct a five-level parking structure behind the old Concourse. New York banks would lend the railroads the $16 million because they held exceptional collateral: not only a solid piece of real estate but also a 25-year government lease of the property, at $3.5 million a year. Uncle Sam, in turn, figured to get its money back (and then some) from parking and concession revenues at the new "National Visitor Center." And, in 2001 for $1 and payment of any back District of Columbia taxes, the government would have the option of buying Burnham's historic edifice.

In 1973, when Interior Department officials were making one of several trips to Capitol Hill in search of supplemental funding, consultant Barry Howard would describe the National Visitor Center as the "foyer of Washington," ready to serve 5,600 or more visitors an hour. As it ultimately developed, National Park Service guides counted themselves lucky if 200 stopped in. As Joe Jensen, a Park Service veteran brought to the project when it got in trouble, would later reflect, "We learned that all roads lead to Rome, but it doesn't necessarily mean that all the *people* go to Rome."

There would be no turning back from plans to tear out the floor of the Union Station Main Hall, in preparation for The Pit. The wholesale renovation of Union Station in the late 1980s would one day restore both the floor and the ornate, two-color marble squares that had onced graced the Main Hall. In railroading's heyday, the basement area to the right housed lockers for Terminal Company workers, a few of whom were known to supplement their brawny jobs with a pad-and-pencil sideline: writing the numbers. The basement floor seen here lay close to ground level on the original Swampoodle site. Burnham & Co. built it up with tons of fill dirt. (National Park Service)

A highlight of tourists' trek through the National Visitor Center was supposed to be a multi-screen slide show, recessed in the old Main Hall floor. The center's manager, Jim Gross, would dub the show the "Primary Audio Visual Experience," or "PAVE." But the hole gouged for PAVE in the old terrazzo floor would soon be immortalized by a less-flattering sobriquet: "The Pit."

"I did not design a pit," architect Auerbach, first hired by the railroads to configure the visitor-center project, would insist in 1988. "I designed a hole in the floor which was to provide access to the lower floor, where all sorts of things, including films, would occur." He said his original plan aimed to avoid cluttering the Main Hall with freestanding exhibits. It called for a glass floor in the basement onto which an orientation map would be projected, visible from that level or from the edges of the breach in the floor above. Lightbursts would show the Tourmobile route and popular Washington attractions. The Auerbach plan also called for ticket centers and information booths on the basement level, reached by escalators. The overall show was intended to say, "This is how you, the visitor, can get around. If you want to learn more, come on down by these escalators. Once you're down there, you can come back up." Visitors were not forced into the basement level, Auerbach said. "If people didn't want to watch this thing, they could just go out the front door." Ultimately when the National Park Service ran short of funds and cut back the envisioned plan, he said, "what they did was put a goddamn wall around the thing and make it a pit—and the escalator became a route to nowhere—so they blew it. What was built [after Auerbach was replaced] was not what was designed."

Richard R. Hite, Interior's controller during the period of the Visitor Center, recalled many years later, "Jim Gross put in this multi-slide show that had waving wheat fields and the like. He went through a lot of mishmash about coming out of the station and seeing the Capitol and having an inspiring experience." PAVE's overall purpose, Barry Howard would tell the Senate, "is to give people a feeling in their throats and in their hearts that Washington philosophically and physically is the center of our nation." Swell, Hite scowled years later, "but most people wanted a place to sleep, bed their family down, get situated."

Robert Peck, a Washington lawyer who was an aide to New York Senator Daniel P. Moynihan when the senator's committee heard a procession of pleas for more money, remembered later: "When the thing opened, I stood there with some tourists and watched these 200-some slide presentations, 10 of which were out at any given moment, flash images of Washington-area landmarks that I could identify, but which the tourists played sort of a guessing game with. It would dissolve to Mount Vernon. People would say, 'White House? Archives?' They'd have no idea." Dick Hite later reflected, "It was really a pretty shoddy effort." Even scaled down, the Pit presentation cost an estimated $1.5 million to design, build and operate.

At first the railroads did little to get the National Visitor Center refitted. They did spend $3.5 million of their own money building a puny "replacement station" under the garage skeleton in back, to handle what everyone thought would be the crumbs of passenger service. But meantime, the Penn Central, successor to the Pennsylvania Railroad as Terminal Company half-owner, had gone bankrupt. Then the highest outbreak of inflation in memory hit the nation. Remembered former Penn Central Board Chairman Robert W. Blanchette in 1988, "We kept saying, every day, 'The garage has to lose a few hundred spaces.' We kept trying to fit the project to the bed, and the bed kept getting smaller." When Interior went to the Senate seeking $8.7 million to finally get construction underway in 1973, the projected garage had shrunk from 4,000 to 2,500 spaces.

But there was no turning back. The department was under the White House thumb to get something done. In his Bicentennial proclamation, President Nixon had called the visitor center "indispensible" and, according to Hite, had "essentially said, 'Rogers Morton [then Interior Secretary], get off your ass and transform this facility.' I remember very well that he [Morton] called me in on a Friday evening. He said, 'Dick, we gotta do something about this Bicentennial proclamation. And now Chessie says, we can't refurbish the station for $16 million. It just can't be done. We've got to get Federal money.' So we went to Congress, and we did get $8.7 million in Federal funds. That's where we, as a Federal entity, got involved with the railroads and their contractor, who were supposed to do the job." Chessie was the Chesapeake & Ohio railroad, which had absorbed the B&O.

According to George B. Hartzog, director of the National Park Service under Stewart Udall, this was the point at which the visitor-center plan began to sour. "I negotiated that contract, so I know what was in it. We weren't going to pay them any damn rent until they put it in condition. . . . Morton and Dick Bodman [his assistant secretary] amended the contract and agreed to pay the railroads rent, at which point [the railroads] said, '[expletive], we got a good deal. We get rent, and we don't have to spend any more money.' Why would [the railroads] want to spend another $10 million to put Union Station in shape when you're already getting $3-million in rent [from Interior] without doing anything?"

Although Morton activated payments to the railroads, his controller, Hite, later took responsibility. "I made that decision," he said. "We were under inexorable pressure to get the daggone thing operative by July 4, 1976. John Collinson [Chessie's chief operating officer] looked us in the eye and said they weren't going to put up another nickel. They weren't going to let us in the building unless we started paying rent." He added, "The choice was to forfeit the whole thing, which would have been totally embarrassing to the Secretary of the Interior and to the President of the United States, or to pay the $3.5 million [a year]. And that was my choice."

"Get the thing done," they did, after a fashion. Said Hite of the Independence Day opening ceremonies, "Ann Armstrong, the counselor to President Ford, was there, and Rog Morton. He had a shovel. I'm not sure what for, since it was already built, but looking at how it turned out, I can guess. We had a big celebration. We literally could not bring in the Marine Band because we were told the roof would fall in from the reverberation." The Main Hall was covered by a cocoa rug, into which $20,000 in cigarette holes would be burned at one inaugural ball alone, five years later.

The National Park Service had longed for a single Washington center at which to orient, Yellowstone-style, the thousands of tourists who arrived in the capital each day. It got its center by reconfiguring Union Station, with unexpectedly disastrous results. In the background is the entrance to the "National Bookstore" in an East Hall room that had once housed the chic Savarin Restaurant. Workers preparing the bookstore stapled cheap carpeting to the elegant marble floor, ruining it; ripped out tapestries and wall fixtures; and painted the tinted marble columns a blazing apartment white. The bookshop sunk to new esthetic depths when water from the center's leaky roof began drenching its volumes. (National Park Service)

The National Visitor Center never got auto or bus parking. Told it would take $4 million more to finish the garage, and weary of his department's parade to the Hill for more money, Interior Secretary Kleppe said, 'No more,' and those few tourists who did happen upon the center and peek out back saw only unfinished steel bones. The city's Metro subway opened a Union Station/National Visitor Center stop, but the line at that time reached only four other close-in locations. Even though manager Gross had told Congress a "tremendous publicity campaign" would be needed to tell visitors the center existed, few, if any, signs could be found on the streets or on the inbound highways of Virginia and Maryland. Recalled Congressman Gray 12 years later, "I went into the Hyatt Regency Hotel, three blocks away, and asked the girl at the desk where the National Visitor Center was. She'd never heard of it."

Train passengers alighting at the front door ran a marathon gauntlet to their trains. They lugged grips and griping youngsters around the Pit in the Main Hall, through a portico to the old Concourse, past displays, then onto a 70-foot concrete road across the gap between the Concourse and the replacement station. From that depot, riders of long-haul trains faced another serpentine tramp up or down more corridors, stairs, and escalators. Back inside, the visitor center's "National Bookstore" and sandwich grill drew few customers. Proprietors of the gift shop stapled plywood over the 1907 marble flooring, destroying it, and painted white the room's natural, tricolor marble columns. Upstairs, where architect Auerbach had envisioned a short-stay hotel and day-care center, mushrooms would sprout in empty and moldering offices. The Park Service moved its archives of thousands of photographs to Union Station, only to have to pack them off again when rain cascaded through the building's aging roof.

Reviews published before, during, and especially after the National Visitor Center's tenure dripped with scorn. They told of disoriented passengers stumbling into the Pit by mistake. One called the building "a torture chamber." In the once-glorious Main Hall, where mahogany benches had been anchored, Charles Ewing of the *Star-News* found multicolored plastic chairs giving "a garish look to the scene . . . like too much rouge on a ruined face." Others wound their way back to Amtrak's train shed and likened it to "Hitler's bunker" and "a small-town bus terminal." Nan Socolow, described by the *Star* as a "poet and gadfly living in Washington," wrote after seeing the visitor center, "What gluttons fed at the pork barrel, leaving something foul and nasty behind at Columbus Plaza? Whoever perpetrated the absolute disaster, the sow's ear, that is the present-day depot should be hung by their heels in a public place.

"Whose idea was it to carpet a railway station? . . . The stains and spots and worn places bring to mind a bum's overcoat."

Senator Moynihan asked Interior Department witnesses if they could assure him that the number of visitors *leaving* the Pit would be the same as the number going in. In a 1980 retrospective series, the *Post*'s Blaine Harden recounted, "Wags . . . have suggested the pit be converted to a disco, an oyster bar, a burial site for Smokey the Bear or a new National Aquarium," utilizing all the water that seeped through the roof. In 1977, the General Accounting Office inspected the building and reported it was heading for a "major structural collapse" unless repairs were made.

The Park Service closed the Pit on Oct. 28, 1978, barely two years after the Primary Audio-Visual Experience had first played; the Visitor Center remained nominally open. In December 1980, leaks in Union Station's roof became unrelenting. Congress eventually authorized another $11 million to plug them, but the contractor was not explicitly instructed to protect the ceiling underneath as repairs proceeded. With the patchwork one-third completed, what was described as a "hundred-year storm" inundated the building, sending chunks of plaster crashing to the floor, ruining what volumes remained in the National Book Store and soaking the carpet. For the luckless Park Service, it never rained but what it poured:

A onetime office of the Washington Terminal Company, abandoned and used for storage during the National Visitor Center occupation, is the worse for water-soaked wear. WTC offices upstairs in the East Hall were never lavish; they were out of public sight, the railroads reasoned, so why gussy them up? When the Union Station Redevelopment Corporation opened one of these rooms to inspect it during the mid-1980s, it found a pile of state flags wadded on the buckled floor. (National Park Service)

Days later, a corroded pipeline burst on the third floor of the west wing, spewing 10,000 more gallons of water. After the center's last activity for Ronald Reagan's inaugural in 1981, the Park Service closed the National Visitor Center for good. Train passengers were shunted outside through a plywood maze to the Amtrak depot. They would not step inside historic Union Station again for nearly eight years.

The project had seemed cursed from the start. Labor strikes bollixed the construction timetable; then, in the rush to catch up and finish, the building's contractor was awarded a "cost-plus" contract that, according to Hite, gave it "no incentive to hurry." Where Interior had been dealing with railroads that were all too happy to downplay passenger service, in 1971 they came face-to-face with Amtrak, a fresh and vigorous crusader for passenger travel. Early on, Amtrak sued to, if not get the great terminal back, at least secure a better replacement depot. Interior and Amtrak squabbled over the National Park Service's desire to close the Visitor Center in off-hours to save on utility costs, which would have forced train passengers outside in the dead of night. "The cart has gotten before what used to be called the 'iron horse,'" Amtrak President Paul H. Reistrup groused. Although the litigation would be withdrawn, the action drove off some of the freight railroads' New York financial backing and fanned already smoldering rancor between Interior and Amtrak's overseer, the Department of Transportation. As Interior's miserable luck would have it, a gasoline shortage hit the nation in the winter of 1973–74, and Amtrak's high-speed Metroliners to New York were catching on — just as the National Park Service was kicking out the trains. Noted William H. Jones of the *Post*, "Like the Australian aborigines, the American passenger train was thought to be doomed. . . . But like the aborigines, who refused to die out, the passenger train has become increasingly popular."

Seven years after the National Visitor Center closed, several key players reflected on what writer E. J. Applewaite, in his book, *Washington Itself*, called, "a berserk memorial to the ineptitude of congressional committees as clients for architectural projects":

Dick Hite: "Well-intentioned people with stars in their eyes kept running on and off stage, saying, 'We're going to do this,' and then Murphy's Law took effect."

Jack Fish, head of the National Capital area region of the Park Service: "It was the best we could expect because of the parking. If it had been there, then I think it would have served the purpose intended. We weren't walking around, hanging our head or anything. The President said get it open, so we had a mission. We gave it our all."

Former Interior Secretary Udall, back practicing law in Arizona: "With the coming of the subway, we thought this was an opportunity to liberate the city from the automobile. The idea was that people could come, park, get this indoctrination, then get on either the subway or the Tourmobile and go out and see Washington, not just drive around in their cars. Not having the parking killed us."

Inspection teams aplenty viewed the water damage at the National Visitor Center. Apparently unworried that additional plaster might tumble, this aggregation is led by Jack Fish, in the raincoat, then deputy director of the National Park Service's National Capital region. The service had moved its nationwide repository of photographs into the National Visitor Center, only to have to move the photos out again when the rains came. (National Park Service)

Gary Heslin of the National Park Service gives a yank to a Union Station mushroom, fungus visitorus centerus, that sprouted in the dankness that followed the inundation, and then the padlocking, of the National Visitor Center. Note the condition of the floor. In other rooms of what had once been a transportation palace, water stood in spreading pools, parquet floors buckled to knee height, and bums and rats set up house. (George Tames/NYT Pictures)

William Walton, arts adviser to President Kennedy and later chairman of the Fine Arts Commission, in retirement in New York City: "The premise was absurd to begin with. You can take tourists away from their cars and put them on trams in a park like Disneyland, but not in a city."

Bill Everhart, who worked at the Park Service's Harpers Ferry, W.Va. "interpretation division" that was summoned to the National Visitor Center to try to make the scaled-down public program palatable: "It's one thing to work at Yellowstone, putting together a film on glaciers and lava flows, and quite another to work in the highly charged political atmosphere of Washington, D.C., where everybody is second-guessing you, taking credit when things go right and pointing fingers when they go wrong. It was a city job in a division that had mostly maintenance people and park police, so everybody ducked when it came time to be assigned there."

Bob Blanchette, who had left Penn Central to become Federal Railroad Administrator and in 1988 was practicing law: "You can be embarrassed in one of two ways. You can decide to solve the problem, or you can let somebody else worry about it. It was an embarrassent to Interior, and they said, 'Let somebody else [DOT] do it.'"

Amtrak's Claytor: "I thought it was stupid, a disaster at the time. We didn't need a visitor center, and to take a terminal and put a hole in it was just asinine. Noboby in transportation wanted to do it. I suspect that the Penn Central and B&O looked upon it as a great way to unload a white elephant."

Lawyer and preservationist Peck: "Events did conspire to make things look worse for Interior. Tastes were just changing when the Visitor Center was being planned. No one had a compunction about what we now consider bad taste, like putting formica on top of marble."

Architect Auerbach, citing Amtrak's litigation and its refusal to accept a road, already designed and funded, to route passengers around back to the replacement station: "They invented the catastrophe that they used to unseat the Visitor Center, because Amtrak wanted back the front door to the Capital. And there you've got the bones of the whole bloody mess. The villains were Amtrak and DOT."

Congressman Gray: "A lot of the stories about 'Gray's White Elephant' have been that there was not a need for a visitor's center. That's absolutely false. The parking garage was the guts of the project, and it never got built. The Nixon Administration failed for a lousy $4 million to finish the garage. Hell, that wouldn't buy a hubcap on a B-1 bomber. If I had it to do over again, as chairman of that committee I'd've just authorized a $25-million parking garage on Capitol Hill, and I'd've been the greatest hero in the country."

Thinking back, Hal Brayman, who was Senate Public Works Committee staff director when Interior Department officials were performing, as Dick Hite later put it, "the typical soft shoe" explaining cost overruns, said he thought Visitor Center designers were right in painting over many of Union Station's classic facades. "But they blew the color," he said. "They should have painted them ken gray."

Water, water, everywhere in frowzy old Union Station, the result of sievelike leaks in the station roof. This photo was taken in the east end of the Concourse, facing the waiting room. When the roof was temporarily dissected and repairs undertaken, a "hundred-year storm" inundated the exposed ceiling and the floors and furnishings below. Cruel critics of the fiasco suggested the rainwater might be useful in The Pit, which could be turned into an aquarium. The revolving doors shown here were later torn out by the Union Station Redevelopment Corporation, which left open the doorway between rooms. (National Park Service)

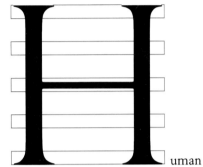

Opposite. During restoration, each section of damaged plaster had to be chipped away, then recast and replaced. Tom Bronson, one of the first Harry Weese & Associates preservation architects on the scene after the terminal had lain empty and mildewing, said the station "looked like something that should have been condemned, and it was about to be." (Carol M. Highsmith, Photographer)

Right. Rehabilitated as part of the restoration of Union Station were the six 25-ton, solid-granite, allegorical statues standing above the arcade along the front of the terminal. This no-nonsense sickle-carrier is Ceres, goddess of agriculture. (Carol M. Highsmith, Photographer)

Human nature drove most politicians and government bureaucrats many arms' lengths from Union Station after it closed. "Success has many fathers, and failure is an orphan," Bob Blanchette would remember in 1988. "As long as the station was a 'hoped-for' success, nobody was having any problems with anybody. The minute it started to go wrong, somebody else was to blame. Nobody wants to be the author of a failure." Even though Dan Rather had just blistered the Visitor Center project on CBS's *60 Minutes* and, as Chief Counsel Mark Lindsey at the Federal Railroad Administration later noted, "no one in Congress had constituents back in their districts jumping up and down, demanding that it be done," two senators, Democrat Moynihan and Republican Robert Stafford, and House Public Works Chairman James D. Howard, stepped forward to champion Union Station anew almost from the moment the National Visitor Center closed. "Unless we want the station to become a ruin, we must do something," Moynihan said.

First, Congress okayed the roof repairs. With plaster hunks resting on the table in front of them, senators had heard Interior's Hite admit he didn't know why the Park Service had not fixed the roof in the first place. "Beats the hell out of me. We were cleaning the eyeballs of the statues and polishing the glass in the skylights, but we didn't fix the damn roof." In 1988 he would add, "Our guy in charge [Gross] was a public-relations guy, not an engineer, any more than I am."

The senators prevailed upon Interior to relinquish the building, and, according to Blanchette, department executives, having endured enough humiliation, were all too happy to agree. "James Watt kept calling Drew Lewis [Blanchette's boss, the Secretary of Transportation] and saying, 'When can I transfer this station over to you?' Drew and I felt it was a magnificent structure, and that the public had been done a terrible disservice with this conversion to something it was never built for. But I kept telling Drew, 'You can't have this thing transferred until you've got a solution in the making.'" After Congress passed the "Redevelopment Act of 1981," authorizing a reconfiguring of Union Station into a reborn railroad station and "marketplace" shopping mall, ala gaudily successful Rouse Co. projects in Boston and Baltimore, DOT commissioned two studies. One certified the building's structural soundness. The other, by the Urban Land Institute, examined options for the old monolith, including rejiggering it as a shopping arcade. Given the legacy of blunders, "the message from Drew Lewis on down," according to Mark Lindsey, was, "'These studies had better be hard-nosed, the answers had better hold up, and the engineering survey had better be encyclopedic.'"

"Graham Claytor was looking to beef up Amtrak's image," remembered Blanchette, "and nothing was worse for its image than that horrible place with mushrooms sprouting from offices. We were assured of support on the Hill; the members of the Senate could look out their windows and see what the Federal Government had wrought upon an unsuspecting citizenry." Noted Lindsey of the FRA, "It was to be Amtrak's headquarters station, in sight of the place from whence its subsidy comes. And it's the station more Americans will see than any other, even if they're not riding the train."

Drew Lewis's successor at Transportation enthusiastically embraced the takeover. "Thank God for Elizabeth Dole," said Amtrak's Claytor in 1988. Mrs. Dole helped find $70-million in Amtrak funds to get the station refurbished. Meantime Charlie Horsky, who later said he felt "Interior really screwed up" at the Visitor Center, was, as he put it, "conspiring" on behalf of an influential business group, the Federal City Council, with City Administrator Tom Downs. "The District has X million dollars in interstate highway money that we can't spend," Horsky later quoted Downs as saying. "We haven't got any plans for it, and it will revert to the Treasury in about 18 months if nothing is done. I think that the District would be willing to put in [what turned out to be $40 million] to finish the garage, and if we finish the garage, maybe we can make something happen." In a sense, the parking garage at a city train station thus became part of the interstate-highway system.

Plaster worker Billy Ford replaces a damaged cap to one of Union Station's Ionic columns. Restoration was a painstaking, laborious process, the results of which are worth pausing to admire. Missing, temporarily, on the wall to the left is one of the many gilded, globed fixtures that adorned the fancier rooms in the mighty terminal. (Carol M. Highsmith, Photographer)

The Pit is just a bad dream as worker John Melton spreads a new concrete base onto the Main Hall floor where the Great Hole of Washington had once yawned. Atop the concrete would come several layers: plastic sheeting to allow the floor to shift and expand slightly, a dry mix into which wire mesh would be laid, two kinds of marble, and grout to secure the tiles in place. (Carol M. Highsmith, Photographer)

Horsky and Lindsey drafted the articles of incorporation for a nonprofit "Union Station Redevelopment Corporation," or USRC, to be chaired by Mrs. Dole. "The first idea was to create another government corporation," Bob Blanchette later remembered. "But we'd had enough of those that were big money-losers: Amtrak, Conrail." In keeping with the new Reagan Administration emphasis on "public-private partnership," "We said, 'Let's do a private company as a convincing demonstration that this wasn't going to be on the public dole.'"

USRC was authorized to return Union Station to railroad service. The historic Concourse became Amtrak's ticketing and baggage facility as well as the three-level "marketplace" center. The Main Hall was set aside as a "restoration space" unsullied by shoe stores and fast-food stalls. In back of the terminal USRC, using those D.C. highway funds, finally completed the parking decks (reduced again to 1,300 auto spaces), a tour-bus level, and the Amtrak waiting and queuing area. The old station's usable space was thus just about doubled, since the original, unheated (and uncooled) Concourse had drawn traffic only at train time.

Amtrak rented the building's upstairs offices as its national headquarters, set about demolishing the tiny "replacement station," and brought the tracks back flush against its new staging area. Now pleased that the railroads had not done the prudent thing and torn down the terminal 30 years earlier, Claytor would say of "the southern terminus of the Northeast Corridor" in 1988, "It's the finest railroad station in the United States again, without any question. Burnham would be proud of it."

The redevelopment agreement called for a $70-million contribution from Amtrak, with the Federal Railroad Administration assuming the yearly lease payments to the railroads under the old Visitor Center deal. The marketplace developers—La Salle Partners, Inc; Williams Jackson Ewing, Inc.; and Benjamin Thompson Associates, selected after national competitions—would pay rent, to rise with inflation and profits, and would split their profits with the government until the Amtrak money was repaid. The new general contractor, the Dick Corporation and the construction manager, Gilbane-Smoot, set to work.

A review board of the city's Council on Historic Preservation approved the project after insisting on modifications to "avoid trivializing" the great building. The developers agreed to reduce four commercial kiosks in the Main Hall to one and to maintain "relatively unobstructed" views of the terminal's lofty ceilings. "People may think we've done violence to the Concourse, when we put three [shopping] levels where only one existed," USRC President Keith Kelly said. "But that was not basically an historic structure. It was a train shed." One highlight of the commercial space would be a "dining room of particular distinction and appeal" in the old presidential reception room.

In a 1982 editorial supporting *modest* redevelopment, the *Post* could not resist a sarcastic look back: "Don we now our hip boots and foul-weather gear for another depressing trip into leaky old Union Station, long the unproud home of not much at all except downpours of water and federal dollars and, it is said, a flourishing rat population." Rodents were not the only nuisance found by the first team of preservation architects to enter the building. Advance teams from Harry Weese & Associates encountered pigeons, chicken bones, human excrement, and, according to project architect Karl Landesz, "bums sleeping down there." Said field architect Tom Bronson, "You'd stand two blocks away and think you were looking at a monument. Inside, it was enough to make you sick. It looked like something that should have been condemned, and it was about to be. It was like a crime had been committed." "Butchery," as they characterized it, from National Visitor Center days included parquet floors buckled three feet high, plaster "in chunks the size of a small room," and the west lobby ceiling "full of holes like swiss cheese."

Left, below. The Barianos family at work in their Rockville, Md., studio. John Barianos—here clearing away imperfections from a newly cast column capital—had applied his restorative skills to projects at the White House, Willard Hotel, Treasury Building and Old Post Office before tackling monumental Union Station. He even talked of one day restoring the ancient Colossus of Rhodes in his hometown in Greece. Joining him in his studio are his wife, Helen, son Vasilios (Bill) and daughter-in-law Irene. The younger generation is casting additional capitals, which will replace those chipped, defaced, or outright lost in Union Station's pathetic period of decline. (Carol M. Highsmith, Photographer)

Left, above. Worker Romero Chavez is wisely secured to a safety belt and rope, since his perch stands 40 feet above the Main Hall floor. One worker did fall to his death during the restoration. Chavez is giving one of Saint-Gaudens' legionnaires a long-overdue bath and facial. Properly placing the soldiers historically has become a Washington cottage industry. They most closely resemble Second Century, A.D., warriors from Gaul, who were mercenaries in the Roman army. You can spot an almost identical helmet on a figure adorning a pack of Gallic cigarettes! The man who modeled for Saint-Gaudens saw the statues at Union Station several years later and pronounced them "pretty crummy." (Carol M. Highsmith, Photographer)

Landesz spent three weeks "just walking the project, getting the feel of what Burnham had in mind." He found a stairway down to the Turkish baths, but no baths; and brickwork inside masonry that does not show on Burnham's plans. Bronson discovered the source of some leaks: "The granite was stacked in layers with no caulking; they had no high-powered sealant like we know of today. The wind blew water into those joints." And he found that "Burnham made a mistake: He designed windows high on the north side of the women's room so that light could pour in. But the sill on those windows is about a foot below the roof outside. Water would collect in the pocket [thus formed] and come on in."

The *Post*'s Jerry Knight would grump in 1983 that he'd had enough of "the boutiquing of America." "There is a finite demand for stuffed wombats, pita bread sandwiches and hanging plants." Still, on March 7, 1984, Interior Secretary William P. Clark signed documents formally transferring jurisdiction of the building to the Transportation Department, and the "mixed-use" redevelopment was on.

So meticulous would be the historic restoration that Weese paint consultant Frank Welsh scraped to find the original 1907 colors of walls. "There were 22 layers of paint in the Main Hall," said Landesz." Frank took a sharp knife and chipped off a cross-section and put it under a microscope, so he could actually read each layer. Once you're down to bare plaster, the first two coats, you figure, are primer, so the third coat out is the original color. But because that color deteriorated over time, he actually scraped *into the middle of that third layer* under the microscope, to match the color using a notation system. Then he could reproduce almost that exact color."

Artist John Barianos, who was charged with restoring everything from Saint-Gaudens' silent sentinels to the intricate Pompeian traceries, went so far as to duplicate Burnham's delicate dying process in creating red-tinted scagliola for the new dining room's marble columns. Washington horologist Elton Louis Howe was commissioned to restore the large east wall clock and two smaller ones. He found that someone, during a "modernization" effort in the 1940s, had junked the clocks' original Magneta Co. workings, clipped out and thrown away internal bulbs, replaced glass covers with plastic, and "worst of all in a Roman building," snapped in clock faces that had Arabic numbers. His recreated clocks featured decidedly Roman numerals.

USRC President Keith Kelly said he endured several interviews in which he was asked, in view of the station's background as a boondoggle: "Are you going to fall on your butt?" No, he responded, the marketplace project would not fail if the six traffic-flow segments (Amtrak passengers, commuter-rail customers, subway riders [estimated by Metro at 15,000 a day at the Union Station stop in 1988], tour-bus visitors, Congressional lunchers, and neighborhood residents) all kicked in, and if the terminal did indeed prove to be the taproot of redevelopment across the eastern end of the city's ceremonial core.

Americans had retained a deep affection for Union Station. Many recalled every detail of shoving off to war there, or falling in love, or just lounging between trains. One man in his 30s, Charles Rich, remembered, as a wide-eyed kindergartner, hurrying with his brother and father into the station's game room to cut a scratchy, five-inch phonograph record on which to wish Mama Rich *bon voyage*. After the National Visitor Center debacle, Washingtonians would confuse the dinky Amtrak depot with "Union Station," but it would not be until 1988, 81 years after the first train pulled out of Daniel Burnham's titanic terminal, that they would again set foot in the *real* Union Station. As they passed through the station's soaring colonnades, they were sure to notice one restoration job above all others: "As fast as we possibly could," said Kelly, "we covered the Pit."

95

A gritty task — turning a sodden, abandoned transportation shrine into a multi-use showplace—fell to the Dick Corporation, contractors and engineers with an eclectic restoration record that ranged from nuclear power plants to the Pennsylvania State Capitol. After poring over architects' drawings, walking "every inch" of the old station, and "best-guessing" what really lay behind peeling walls, 25 separate roofs, and massive columns, Dick honed a bid to the nearest $100. A "crap shoot," a bid-team member called it, so many were the unknowns. Acceptance of President David E. Dick's $48,310,500 bid by the Union Station Redevelopment Corporation in 1986 set loose a pressure-packed race to meet a deadline for a candlelight reopening gala scarcely two years away.

More than 300 craftsmen bent to Project Superintendent Gene Butler's direction amid a blur of dust and a caterwauling of saws, mixers and jackhammers. In the frantic final week in early September 1988, the number would swell to more than 800 — European artisans, American journeymen, even sweep-up laborers recruited from Washington halfway houses.

Dick's task was prodigious: covering and re-shoring The Pit; dropping the basement floor five feet to accommodate theaters, cafes, and baggage handling; installing new, concealed heating-and-cooling ductwork. Crews tearing into shafts never before opened unveiled a bonanza of collectibles: 1905 bottles, newspapers, spoons, pepper cans, and even a hand-carved, 6-ft. propellor that had likely been part of a crude cooling system. The latter-day contractors practically had to redesign as they went, firing off more than 1,000 urgent "RFIs" — requests for information — to architects and historical researchers as they poked into crannies theretofore unrevealed.

Left. Another "train through the wall" story with a happier twist was the clever shop entrance to one of the terminal's most appropriate new tenants: the Great Train Store. (Carol M. Highsmith, Photographer)

Right. Notice anything odd in this photo of horologist Elton Howe and his grand restoration of an old Main Hall clock? The "IIII" was not only faithful to Burnham's original, it was also standard Roman until well into the 20th Century; so was "VIIII" for "IX." The yellow line arcing across the clockface is not a crack or imperfection. It's a reflection of gold leaf glinting from the ceiling above. (Carol M. Highsmith, Photographer)

Bushhammer operators ran into a massive metal deck and concrete slab where the Federal Express of '53 had burst through the Concourse floor. Electricians struggled to trace conduits buried in granite walls. They'd shoot them full of soapy water to loosen 83-year-old, coagulated wiring, hoping to see a spray of suds burst, somewhere, out the other end. Often the liquid *never* emerged, so whole new conduits had to be cut in joints between granite slabs. Experts argued whether a shadowy effect in an old, black-and-white photo of the Presidential Suite was a deliberate "leathering look" fashionable at the time, or an accident of reflected lighting. The leathering effect won the day, and Dick artisans sponged layers of mottled-brown paint and lacquer onto the final canvas.

As they carved three shopping levels into the open-air Concourse, tearing out some girders and shoring up others, workers struggled against an imposed 100-pounds-per-square-foot weight limitation. Drywall could not be stacked, steelmovers could not skitter across floors, concrete could be mixed in small batches only. Dick engineers devised an elaborate "crawler" system in which a crane walked itself down the Concourse, reaching behind it as it went to pick up and redeposit mats that spread the weight. Once, machinery lifted the entire east "window wall" so that beams underneath could be strengthened, yet broke not a pane. In the alcove between the plaster ceiling and the many rubber-membrane roofs installed in Interior's damage-control frenzy of 1981, workers suspended from lifelines attached to trestles took care not drop a wrench or putty knife, lest it crash through the delicate plaster ceiling to the floor 90 feet below.

Project Manager John T. Sebastian supervised this contractor's beehive. "In the winter, we had to get heat into the building so the painting; stenciling, canvassing and plastering would 'take,'" he noted. "There were no functioning utilities, so we set up boilers on semi-trailers outside that pumped 12-million b.t.u. into that building."

Few feats of restoration could match, for pure persistence, the saga of the Concourse ceiling glass, half of which had been shattered over time and needed replacing. Senior Project Manager Don F. Cooper, who lived the story from South Korea to eastern Tennessee, held in his hand a square of glass, ⅜" thick, etched with Florentine swirls and laced with protective chicken wire: typical safety glass of Burnham's day. Cooper soon determined it had been crafted by Pittsburgh Plate Glass in 1904, and it seemed simple enough to duplicate for the 10,000-or-so square feet of ceiling that needed reworked.

Cooper picked up the tale of what became a maddening Union Station scavenger hunt: "It was a common kind of rolled glass, but PPG quit making it in 1912. You could go down to any hardware store and find wire mesh, but not that fine a pattern, and it would be made of the wrong kind of material. This was a special alloy to which molten glass would adhere. I called every steel manufacturer, told 'em I'd pay extra money to re-create that process, that I'd buy 10 times more than I needed. They said no, no way.

Daniel Burnham's passion for natural light is again rewarded in the enticingly remodeled West Hall. Sunbeams stream through Burnham's skylights in this view, looking east toward the Main Hall, turning the old ticketing and baggage-checking alcove into a sunny, upscale shopping arcade. (Carol M. Highsmith, Photographer)

The Presidential Suite lost none of its early elegance when artisans remade the space into the fashionable Rattlesnake Club restaurant. Specs throughout the building called for gold leaf, not just gold paint, and more than 70 pounds of leafing were delicately applied. At gold prices current in the late 1980s, that Midas touch represented an almost-$500,000 investment. (Carol M. Highsmith, Photographer)

"In Belgium, I finally found one steel person that supplies all the wire that goes into every piece of glass in the world. He'd quit doing that chicken-wire pattern two years ago. He, too, said he couldn't retool just to make the little bit we needed. We literally searched warehouses all over the world for six months, hoping someone had stuck away some of that wire. Finally we found a guy someplace who said, 'We had a roll of that; let me go out and check.' He came back and said, 'Yeah, we had the form, but we loaded it out three months ago, sent it to the dump.' That's how close we came to getting the wire.

"Then there was that distinctive swirl pattern. We finally found a guy who said, 'Yeah, there was a plant down in Louisiana that would roll that kind.' We went down there, and the plant had been disassembled five years ago; couldn't find any machinery or anybody who might have kept it as a souvenir. We called manufacturers of patterned glass all over the world—Italy, Korea, even a place in India—nothing. We ended up going to an art place in Indiana that makes glass for shower stalls and tiffany lamps. Somebody there said he got the patterns from a toolmaker in New Jersey. So I trucked up to New Jersey, and we found two or three old people who knew how to roll out a piece of this glass using acid. So we got the roller, the pattern.

"The art-glass place couldn't roll it; it couldn't control the temperature enough to get a consistent pattern. So we went down to Kingsport, Tennessee, to AFG Industries. Twenty-four hours a day, they run patterns for huge national retailers. I practically begged them to run our pattern. They said, 'We shut down for only six hours a *year.*' I explained the Union Station project, really sold its historic value, said they could put the fact that they helped us in their brochure! Finally they relented, and they made the glass we needed.

"But we still didn't have the wire. We tried everywhere, and it just couldn't be done. What we ended up doing was laminating this new, patterned glass to safety glass, to insure safety. In Kingsport, I noticed that they were putting designs on the glass —literally painting on decorations. I said, 'Why don't we *paint* the wire pattern! We don't need the wire for safety.' We found some little old guy who was willing to give it a try, and it worked. So we virtually created a whole new technology for historic glass. It took a year and a half, and we didn't get the last shipment until a week before Grand Opening, but the job got done. Now half the [Concourse] ceiling is original glass, half is this new product that took us 18 months to put together, and you can't tell the difference."

A dedicated train buff, madcap weatherwatcher Willard Scott of NBC's "Today Show," emceed Union Station's gala re-opening. Grand pianos tinkled, newsboys in knickers hawked an "extra," pasty-gray human models of Saint-Gaudens' statues posed, and tap-dancers decked out as a snaking model train did temporary violence to John Barianos's new marble floor. (Carol M. Highsmith, Photographer)

Sebastian, too, had been problem-solving. When plans for a new heating and cooling plant underneath the terminal were scuttled for lack of space, he arranged to tap into the Architect of the Capitol's steam and chilled-water supplies as far as three blocks away.

Looking back, wistfully, while preparing to leave Washington for another, less-epic assignment, Sebastian reflected, "Union Station has been a bit like raising a child and having to send it off on its own. It was exhilarating, especially at Grand Opening, when people seemed impressed that we'd raised the child correctly. But it's also a hollow feeling, having to move on." Cooper, too, waxed philosophic. He said, "Our hope is that, 80 years from now, when people go to restore this building again, they'll be able to come back to the work we did, go through our research and records and patterns that we used to re-create 1907, and have a solid base from which to again perpetuate the inspiration of Daniel Burnham. Like him, maybe we were able to stop time for a moment."